HOW TO MARKET A BOOK

BY LORI CULWELL AND KATHERINE SEARS

A simple guide to "Do-It-Yourself" marketing and publicity for your book, including websites, social media, and traditional PR outreach.

Edited by Janna Balthaser

Cover Design by Greg Simanson

ISBN: 978-1-935961-31-4
EPUB ISBN: 978-1-62015-035-1

DISCOUNTS OR CUSTOMIZED EDITIONS MAY BE AVAILABLE FOR EDUCATIONAL AND OTHER GROUPS BASED ON BULK PURCHASE.

For further information please contact info@booktrope.com

Library of Congress Control Number: 2012905189

DEDICATION

LORI

Stephan Cox is the origin of all awesomeness in the universe.

KATHERINE

To Tobin and Taryn - who never mind that my nose is perpetually in a book.

TABLE OF CONTENTS

Intro: Who Are We? What Can We Teach You? 7

Part One: The Setup 11

Chapter 1: What's This All About, Anyway? 12

Chapter 2: Write a Good Book! 17

Chapter 3: Get Your Toolkit Ready 21

Chapter 4: Whip Your Website Into Shape 26

Chapter 5: Set Up Social Media Profiles 38

Chapter 6: Get on the Book Sites 43

Part Two: Get on Out There! 59

Chapter 7: Blogging /Networking 60

Chapter 8: Search Engine Optimization:
Keywords and Content and Metadata, Oh My! 74

Chapter 9: Your Social Media To-Do List 80

Chapter 10: What to Do on the Book Sites 88

Chapter 11: Talk It Out! 95

Chapter 12: Traditional PR.......................... 108

Bonus Material 123

Intro: Who are we? What can we teach you?

Lori Culwell: Author, Marketer, Tech Nerd

Hi there! I'm Lori Culwell. In case you've never heard of me (that's fine, I'm not Stephen King), let me introduce myself. I am a writer, I own an internet company, and I have a blog called Funny Strange. I write for the Huffington Post, my work was once nominated for a Pushcart Prize, and I have consulted on SEO (search engine optimization) for some of the biggest websites in the world.

Also, I hold the noteworthy distinction of being one of the few people in America who can say they wrote a fiction novel, self-published it, and sold so many paper copies, Simon & Schuster bought it and re-released it.

Yep, it happened. Here's the story in case you want to know more about it or are dying to read the novel (hey, who am I to stop you?): http://www.loriculwell.com/novel/.

Because this accomplishment (which occurred with no eBooks whatsoever) made me something of a self-publishing unicorn, I still get interviewed and asked about it to this day. Every last person I talk to about this thinks that there was some big secret involved, or that I knew someone, or that I used magic and voodoo to sell all those books.

I am here to tell you, there was no magic, and no voodoo. I am not related to anyone at Simon & Schuster, and in fact, when I self-published, the agent I was working with dropped me like I was a publishing hot potato. Nope, when I marketed that book there was just me, sitting in front of the computer with the singular mission of finding my audience, even if I had to do it one person at a time.

In fact, I will tell you something even MORE shocking—once the novel found a home at Simon & Schuster, I did just as much marketing as before. Yes, I had a larger platform and more people were willing to talk to me, but I thought it was really interesting that there was just as much work at the "end of the publishing rainbow" as the beginning. Since then I've written four other books and helped with marketing for authors, agents, and publishing houses. I even have a whole news-type website that's dedicated to this topic: http://www.bookpromotion.com.

Along the way I made some (ok, a lot) of notes, and those notes eventually turned into this guide, which I hope will help you achieve a publishing success story of your own. The truth is, once you get the marketing ball rolling, it's actually empowering! Oh, and if you need encouragement, I'm on Twitter at http://twitter.com/loriculwell. I would also love to hear your success stories, because I am 100% positive you can do it. After all, you're smart and dedicated—you wrote a whole book! Not only should you be proud of yourself, but you should want to tell the world, getting the book out there to as many people as possible.

KATHERINE SEARS: BOOK MARKETING MAVEN

Unlike Lori, I am not an author. In point of fact, this is the first book I have ever written. What I am, is a marketing person and co-founder of Booktrope— a totally new kind of publishing company. Feel free to check us out for more details at http://booktrope.com. We have published more than a hundred books, our books routinely appear in Top 100 lists on all the popular online retailers globally (on one day in February 2013 we were on 65 of them) and our top selling book, (*Riversong* by Tess Thompson) is approaching 100K copies sold. In other words, we practice what we/I preach at Booktrope, and while nothing is fool-proof, I can assure you that persistence beats inactivity every time.

My background is in technology and internet marketing, and most recently, books. Why is this important? Well, I happen to think that marketing books is really no different than any other sort of marketing, or rather it shouldn't be. It was a different animal when there was no internet and you could only buy books in a bookstore. But in today's world of Kindle, Nook, blogging, and social media, those old tried (or maybe I should say tired) and true standards just do not apply anymore. If you are going to be successful today, you need to do more than just write a great book. In fact, even if you write a great book, you'll still need to put some effort into getting yourself and that book out into the world.

Let's talk names and numbers.

- Facebook© 1 billion (with a b!) people now use Facebook. More than 30 billion pieces of content are shared each day, and Facebook generates a staggering 1 trillion (with a t!) views per month.
- Twitter© As of 2012, Twitter had 500 million users, and that number increases by 300,000 every day.
- Reddit© Regularly surpasses 2 billion page views per month.

- LinkedIn© LinkedIn adds a new user every second, which as of the end of 2012, was 200 million.
- Book Bloggers There are more than 4,000 bloggers online today.
- Goodreads© Gets 19 million monthly unique visitors, 140 million monthly page views, and 100,000 new users a month.
- Amazon© It's the 5th most popular website in the world and has more than 5 million books on its site at any given time.

That's a lot of people—surely some of them would enjoy reading your book, right?

Are you involved with all of those yet? You should be on at least a few (if not all) of them. And in case you're wondering, the above is by no means an exhaustive list; the internet is a smorgasbord of free marketing opportunities. But don't panic. That's what this book is about—helping you understand which tools you need for YOUR book and how to use them. So without further ado (I have always wanted to use the word *ado*), let's begin!

PART ONE: THE SETUP

First off, we're going to just give you a little overview of what book marketing is all about, debunk some myths, and give you some examples of people just like you who have used marketing to achieve amazing things. Next, we'll help you pull your tools together, assemble them in website form, get set up on social media and book sites, and form a plan of attack. Don't get overwhelmed—it's a step-by-step process, and you've taken a great first step in buying this book! We'll give you screenshots along the way, and when something is even more complicated, you'll see this symbol:

This means we have more tools for you over on the BookPromotion.com site. Just click the link next to the tools to see what we're talking about!

Basically, what you want marketing and publicity to do is build **momentum** behind your book, and to make it easy for people to find you and your work. You want people to get excited about your book so they'll recommend it to their friends, share it on Facebook and Twitter, and suggest it to their book clubs. You want to point everyone back to your website so that more people can love your writing and buy your books. Having a website and some social media presence will make you feel good about the fact that you have a clear mission and you're acting on your own behalf every day, and it will be great for your "reputation management," meaning what people find when they Google you. Marketing and publicity don't have to be scary or arduous if they become part of your daily routine, and as a creative person, you owe it to yourself to get your work out there. You worked really hard on that book—make sure it has a chance!

1
WHAT'S THIS ALL ABOUT, ANYWAY?

We know what you're thinking.

Well, maybe we don't know EXACTLY what you're thinking. We're not psychics—just a couple of girls who have been in the publishing/marketing game a long time, so we've looked at this situation from every angle and we have some pretty good insight.

Back to what you're thinking.

If you've finished your book and it's published (either through a traditional publisher or self-published), first of all, congratulations! Getting your book out there is a big deal!

You are probably now exhausted, and the thought of doing marketing and publicity makes you want to collapse in a heap on top of your computer. We understand. It takes tremendous effort to write a book, then (the part they don't tell you) even MORE effort to get it out there, to brave the daily rejection of agents and publishers only to hear, "Not interested, sorry!" over and over again. It breaks your heart a little every time, so when you finally find a home for your book and turn your manuscript in, you are DONE. You don't want to think about that book anymore, you're ready for a break, and frankly, who can blame you?

We acknowledge 100% that writing is hard, editing is hard, and getting your book to a publisher (or self-publishing) is *really* hard. The whole thing makes you feel like a wrung-out washcloth, which is why, frankly, many books do not succeed. We've heard this from many authors—once the book comes out, they feel like marketing and publicity are someone else's job, that they shouldn't HAVE to do it, don't know HOW to do it, or don't have the ENERGY to do it. Myths, all of them! Let's talk about them one at a time.

Myth #1: "It's Not My Job."

We believe the overall lack of success of most authors' books is due to one simple reason: Authors think that the process is OVER once the book is published, when really, that's when it's just beginning. Most authors feel like they're running a race, and when they turn that book in, they've reached the finish line. The dirty secret that most authors aren't told (or maybe just don't acknowledge) is that the book publishing process is a marathon, and turning in the book is mile 13 (halfway, in case you don't run marathons).

This information is not meant to be daunting—rather, this whole guide's purpose is to give you not only the real truth about what it takes to sell books, but tools and steps that you can take to do just that. You like writing, right? You must be pretty good at it, or else you wouldn't have gotten this far. Our job is to make sure that you finish the race, making sure that you do the marketing necessary to sell books and get people excited about your work so that you (you guessed it!) may get more contracts to write more books in the future.

Just to touch briefly on the "marketing is the publishing company's job" myth. It's true that if your book is with a big publisher, there IS a publicist that works there, and they probably will do some work on behalf of your book. But (and this is nothing against you, you're awesome, you wrote a book!) let's be honest—that publicist works for a big publisher, and so most of his/her job is probably spent on authors like Dan Brown and David Sedaris, who have name recognition and will sell a ton of books just by appearing on talk shows.

No, it's not fair, but this is the way the publishing world works. If you want to be a big-name author who sells big-time books and you don't happen to already be famous, you'd better get to work building up your Twitter following—or writing blogs, or sending out press releases and review copies, or any (and all!) of the other things we're going to tell you about in this guide.

Myth # 2: "I'm Going to Hire a Publicist, So I Don't Need to Be Involved."

If you have the resources to hire someone, or are with a publisher that DOES provide you with a more dedicated individual, awesome! BUT you will still have to do the vast majority of what is in this book (like setting up your website and social media), and the more you know about the process of what the publicist is doing, the better.

Why? There are two key reasons.

1 Because no matter how great that person is at marketing (we speak from experience on this), they cannot take the place of you, the person who wrote the book. Readers want to know what YOU think. They want to know what made YOU write your book, what you're about, and what makes you enjoy life, and they want to hear YOUR voice. There is only so much of this another person can communicate on your behalf and still seem real or relatable.

2 Because even if you are paying someone good money to help you market your book, you must still know what is going on so you'll know if they are actually doing what they are supposed to do. Knowledge is

power, and you never want to give away all of your power. Just ask now-broke athletes or people who trusted Bernie Madoff with their entire financial futures.

Also—and this is something publicists are hesitant to discuss—the services of a publicist are actually only REALLY helpful if your book happens to be newsworthy or related to a current topic/news story. Here's something they WON'T tell you—if you have your website/social media set up properly, by the time a news story breaks, you will already be known to be an authority in your subject, so you won't need the publicist to connect the dots.

Myth # 3: "I'm Too Scared."

Another thing we hear a lot is that writers are terrified of marketing. They don't know how to do it. They majored in something creative in college, like Dance or Theater or English, and therefore did not acquire the requisite business skills to one day become a marketing expert.

If this is you, then we have good news for you. Despite what you might have heard, marketing is not NEARLY as hard as writing a book. It's actually much easier.

In fact, here is an "Aha!" moment for you: Marketing is not a mysterious art form. Mostly, marketing is just writing, but with a specific purpose and direction, directed at people who could spread the word about your work/become your fans/help with your career. If it helps, you can think of marketing like planting seeds every day: some of those seeds are going to go nowhere, and some of them are going to take root and grow into flowers. You don't necessarily know what's going to happen with each seed, but you spend time every day tending the garden, right?

Since you wrote a whole book and are already an expert in your field, and you now have a step-by-step guide of things you can and should be writing next, we are crowning you "honorary marketing expert."

Marketing can take the form of chatting with people on Twitter every day, or writing blogs, or sending your book out to reviewers. Marketing can take the form of being an expert on radio and TV shows, and who wouldn't like that? In fact, marketing (this might shock you) IS ACTUALLY ENJOYABLE. It is awesome when your book sales go up, when someone contacts you to tell you they stayed home from work because they simply could not put down your novel, or when a group of people reads your book for their weekly book club, and contacts you to come and speak to them about it. Awesome!

Myth # 4: "It's Too Hard, and I Don't Know Where to Start."

Ok, this is a valid point—getting everything set up so that your marketing machine runs smoothly CAN be a daunting task, and it can require learning some new things if you've considered yourself a Luddite/technophobe in the past. If it's any consolation, you will only have to do things once—like setting up your website—and then the pain of that will be over and you'll have something you're proud to send people over to, because you'll know it's helping you sell books.

So—yes, there will be some new things to learn, but we believe you can do it! After all, you wrote a whole book, so we are confident that one website and some social media profiles are not going to get the best of you, no matter how initially frustrating they might be to understand.

Also, we talked to hundreds of writers in the preparation of this guide, so we have tried to make it as easy as possible to get yourself up and running without getting stuck. We hear you. You want to be a writer, not a web designer/social media expert! We promise to help you get set up as easily as possible.

Just so you know what we're going to be talking about, here is a brief overview of what an author needs to have these days:

- An author website (www.firstnamelastname.com) which contains a blog and has pertinent information about you and your work, and most especially, a clickable image of your book that appears on every page. When clicked, this book should lead the user to your favorite bookseller where they can purchase your book. The purpose of this website is to quickly give potential readers more information about you, to provide samples of your writing, and (most importantly) to connect them with your book.

- Profiles on social media like Twitter, Facebook, and Google Plus—all of which link back to your main author website where people will be encouraged to find out more about you and ultimately find and buy your book.

- Author profiles on book sites like Amazon, BN.com, Shelfari, Goodreads, and LibraryThing, all of which (again) link back to your main author website where potential readers can easily find and buy your book.

Once you have these elements set up, you can spend time on whatever social media platform appeals to you, and participate in topic-related forums online with the goal of establishing yourself as an expert and driving people back to your website so that they start following your work and ultimately buy your books.

Did we mention we want people to buy your books?

If you're feeling sad or unmotivated about self-promotion, please drop by and visit BookPromotion.com, where you can find stories about people who succeeded and how they did it, plus news and tools. We're here for you!

2
WRITE A GOOD BOOK!

Perhaps this goes without saying, and we certainly don't want to belabor this point or offend anyone, but we want to be sure we cover all the bases in this guide. We're not trying to tell you how to write, what to write, or even how to pick the genre in which you want to write. Write what you want, we say!

In the future (and especially after reading this guide and interacting with your target audience a little bit), you might find yourself starting your next book in response to market research or topics that your readers tell you they want to know about. If/when you start doing this, you will find that it's a little easier to do your marketing, since you've already got an engaged market of readers who told you what they wanted.

You'll also find it's actually easier to write a good book when readers tell you what exactly they want to know. That's a different discussion for a different guide, though. We're talking about the book that you were inspired to write—the book that you stuck with and finished, and that you're now going to put out into the world.

We're also not trying to tell you how to publish. If you've sold your book to a traditional publisher and are in the midst of the editing process, congratulations! That is fantastic, and since the publisher will provide you with an editor who will help you make the book better, you are almost certain to end up with a book that you'll be proud of and confident to promote. You're also not going to have a lot of choice when it comes to editing, proofreading, and design, so feel free to skim this chapter and move on to the next. If you're going to self-publish or your book is with a smaller publisher where you might be participating in the process a little more (and no judgment—sometimes self-publishing/indie press is the way to go!), there are just a few areas in which you're going to need to be a little more diligent in order to ensure that your book is the best it can be.

Now we need to be a little bit blunt: If you do not have a good book, you can put massive effort into your marketing, and you're probably not going to see the stellar results that we've cited as example. Some people don't take our advice—they self-publish without the benefit of editors, designers, or proofreaders, pour their energy into marketing, and then end up disappointed.

We don't want to see that happen to you, so we'll give you just a few basic steps you can take to ensure that what you've written is "good," although we agree, there are some bestsellers that aren't very "good," and the very concept of "good" is pretty subjective anyway.

First off: Get feedback!

Let's cut to the chase, people: You (as a writer) are a business, and your book is a product, and as such, it needs to be high quality. Before you start trying to sell a book, you need to let some people actually read that book—preferably more than ten people, and preferably people who are as honest as possible. If you have to join a writer's group or take a class to get honest feedback, do it. You must let some people who are not your friends (or your mom) read your book before you offer the book for sale or do any sort of marketing effort. This can probably not be emphasized enough. You need feedback (and plenty of it) to shape your book into the stellar product you know it can be, and if you do not get it before you start marketing, you are going to end up getting it anyway—from angry and disgruntled readers, in the form of snarky emails and mean reviews on Amazon. This "tough love" is not meant to scare you away from writing—rather, it is meant to scare you into action, to go out and get some feedback on what you've written.

Here is what we think "good book" means, and hopefully what your test readers will tell you:

- It must be well written. We don't care how, when, or where you learn to write, but you do need to learn the basic rules of the craft, and learning the craft of writing involves not only writing, but reading—a lot of reading. In fact, we're told that the motto of one writing program is, "Read 100 good books. Write one." Once you know the rules, you can break them, but doing so by accident rarely turns out well. Sign up for a writing class if you're not confident, or get into a writer's group, or form a group of readers/writers on your own so you can get regular feedback and keep each other honest on your deadlines.

- It should conform (mostly) to its genre. Again, once you know the rules, you can break them. But readers are a loyal crowd when it comes to genre (we will talk more about genre later). So, if you break those rules, just know that you may alienate some of those readers. In other words, if you do it, do it intentionally and with full knowledge that you are doing it! This goes back to the above point: know your craft. If you haven't already, find or form a group of writers who love this genre and who are honest enough to tell you that the "shoot 'em up car chase" scene you wrote does not belong in your women's fiction novel.

-   It must be edited by someone other than you. Whether that means you hire someone (if you are an independent author) or whether an editor is part of your contract (with a publisher), this is a step that cannot be skipped.

-   It must be proofread by a professional. This is usually a secondary step in the editing process, but it cannot (must not!) be overlooked. Yes, it is true that most books (even from big publishers) end up with a typo or two. But don't let your inaction or inattention to this step be the cause of that problem, because it is really painful when your Amazon reviews are based on your readers' animosity toward the amount of typos in your book and not on the merit of the story itself.

-   It must have a professional cover. If your book is with a traditional publisher, you will have little to no control over this phase. If you are independent, or with a smaller press, do NOT skip this critical step. Spend the time, money, and effort to make this a perfect first impression for your book. You never get a second chance at that first glance (yes, it does sound corny, but admit it, you will remember it)! Keep in mind that since e-books are taking over, the way your book cover looks as a thumbnail is probably more important than how it looks full size, since most of your readers will have already purchased it before seeing it "live," plus most of your readers will be reading it in digital format anyway.

-   It must have an appealing and informative back cover. Despite the fact that many people will see it live for the first time once they have already purchased it, the material on the back cover is frequently used elsewhere, such as for your Amazon and Barnes & Noble .com descriptions. It needs to give someone a desire to read your book, pure and simple. So whether that includes author blurbs, your bio, or just the book description is really between you and your publisher. But whatever is there, make it clear, compelling, and professional.

Once your book has gotten enough feedback, has been through a thorough editing and proofreading process, and has a professional cover design, you will feel confident in your marketing—because you'll know what you have to offer is great. Don't rush it!

3
GET YOUR TOOLKIT READY

First things first! Let's get right in there and deal with the most basic weapons in your marketing arsenal—a decent photo of you, plus some biographical information and a little analysis of your competition. First make a new folder in your email or on your desktop where you can keep all of this stuff so it's readily available to you—and so you don't waste your precious marketing time hunting for photos, your bio, or a summary of your book every time someone asks for one of these.

Right now, let's gather the elements that you will need in order to get your website and social media profiles together. Put together some information about you and your book (including an image of the book cover), a photo of you, and some examples of your writing. We're going to put all of this into a folder on your desktop so it's easily accessible.

Getting all of these simple components organized at this point in the process will save you time and hassle when you're doing other things that might actually be challenging, like pulling your website together. Let's prepare to win!

First off, make a new folder on your desktop. Call it "Book Promotion" so it will be easy to find. In it you will put the following elements:

YOUR BIO AND BACKGROUND INFORMATION

You probably already wrote one of these for your book (like for the book jacket), and if so, go ahead and dig that up right now. In case you haven't done this yet, here's what should go into a bio: your name, writing experience, and any work experience that pertains to your book (like if you wrote a diet book and you're a certified nutritionist). Different PR venues, websites, and social media destinations might want different lengths for this, so prepare a version that's 250 words as well as 100 words. Even if you don't have your website set up yet, make a note to always include a reference in your bio that takes people back to your main website where they can buy your book. Also, write down (for your own notes) your hometown, home state, and the location of the book you've written if that pertains to your book at all. Later, you might want to refer to this list quickly when you're looking for media venues who might want to feature your book, and we want you to have everything handy!

YOUR PHOTO

Right now, find the author photo you used on your book cover, or if you don't like that one or can't find it, find a photo of yourself that you can live with, and save a copy of it into the "Book Promotion" folder on your desktop. You should have this handy because bloggers, reviewers, or newspaper people often want a photo to go along with something they write about you (or guest posts you will write). You're also going to want a decent photo of yourself for your social media profiles, and you'll need to put a photo of yourself on your website so people can see that a real person wrote your book. If you don't have a suitable recent photo of yourself that would be appropriate for promoting your book, set up a photo session with a friend who is good with a camera or with a professional photographer. Get this one off your list now—you will thank us later!

Side note: Authors sometimes ask if it's ok if they use an image of their book cover in their social media, on their websites, and in their professional communications. Our professional opinion is "no," for several reasons. Since this guide is all about empowering you with the tools to act on your own behalf, we will give you those reasons, and then you are free to make your own decision about this subject.

First off, remember that you are marketing your book, but ultimately, you are marketing yourself and your writing. On social media, for instance, it is very strange for a book to be having a conversation on Twitter. This creates cognitive confusion in people's minds, and confusion does not help you sell more books.

Another reason we don't recommend it is that, depending on how you're using the book cover image, you might be violating Facebook's Terms of Service. This applies to the specific instance of replacing the image of your personal profile with an image of your book's cover, and using this for promotional purposes. Once you do this, you have crossed over into the realm of "using personal profile for business gain," and if Facebook catches you doing this, they are within their rights to turn off your entire profile and take away all of your friends. Don't become alarmed—we will talk much more about social media properties in later modules, and it is very simple to make a Facebook Fan Page, both for yourself and your book. For now though, the main point is this: If all you have is a Facebook profile, please use a photo of yourself (and not your book) in that profile. So go on, find a great photo of yourself and save it in the folder. This will save you approximately 9,000 minutes when you don't have to hunt for the photo every time someone asks for it.

Book Summary

Sounds simple enough, right? If you're done with the editing process, you can simply go over to your book jacket or your book's inside flap and copy what's there. We might also call this the "elevator pitch" for your book, or how you would describe your book if you were riding in an elevator with someone. You should also put some time into composing a summary of why exactly you wrote your book, as well as what the book is about.

You will need a great summary of your book for multiple marketing uses along the way, from the "About this Book" page on your own blog to the bio you provide for any guest blogs you might do. Write it down and memorize it so you'll be prepared anytime someone says, "Oh, you wrote a book? What's it about?"

You should take a little time to make longer and shorter versions of this summary, as some bloggers/reviewers/newspaper people/websites might allow you to say more (in which case you totally should!). You will need the biographical information (both long and short form) for social media profiles, for your website, and for other unforeseen circumstances along the way.

Links and Logins

If your book is out, go and grab the link from Amazon, Barnes & Noble, or wherever you would like people to buy it. Put this link into a Word file, along with the URLs for any social media you might already have (like your Twitter handle, for instance). Also, make note of the user name/password for each account so you don't waste time looking for these every time you want to start some social media outreach. Prepare to succeed!

If you're a "write it down" kind of person, we've provided a worksheet where you can answer all of these questions, over at http://bookpromotion.com/tools. Go get it!

Notes on Your Target Audience

You already did this as you were writing your book, but right now, take a minute to make some notes about the types of people you wrote it for, like "stay-at-home moms" or "geologists." These notes will come in very handy once you're up and running and ready to reach out to websites, groups, or publications.

Which brings us to your next task: It is time to identify your specific target audience. These are the people you actually believe will read and enjoy your book. This bears repeating —not just the people who *could* read your book, the people who will **read it and enjoy it**. Your goal with marketing is not just to blast the readers out there with your title, it is to find the specific group of people who are already pre-disposed to like your book, and tell them about it. All of the work you just did (key words, genres, etc.) will now help you decide who your target audience is. Everything else you do from here on out is to be done keeping this audience in mind.

To add to your ever-growing group of lists, let's make one about your book. At the top, put all the genres you came up with. Then write down a list of words or themes that you think are present in your book.

Notes on Your Category

You already also considered this when writing your book, but let's clarify it further and put it in this folder, just so we know. Think of it this way: What section of the bookstore would your book go in? Is it a cookbook? Women's fiction? Personal development? Make a few notes on this, just so you're perfectly clear on where your book fits in the big picture.

Notes on the Competition

As you get started, it will be very helpful for you to see who else is out there—not so that you get intimidated, but to give you ideas for what other people who have books similar to yours are doing. For this, you'll take the competitive analysis you did when you wrote your book proposal. (If you haven't already done a competitive analysis, go over to Amazon.com and research the top ten books in the category that you identified above.) Look at the top ten self-help/women's fiction/cookbooks/memoirs/etc. and write down everything about each of them: the author, what the predominant color or theme of that genre seems to be, and anything else that stands out.

Make notes on authors who have great websites or large Twitter followings. You will be referring to this list later!

NOTES ON HOBBIES OR INTERESTS THAT PERTAIN TO YOUR BOOK OR GENRE

Here are some questions that will help:
- What is the genre of your book?
- Is this your favorite genre?
- Who are your favorite authors?
- Does this have relevance in your personal life? Example: If you wrote a medical drama, are you a doctor or nurse? What made you so interested in medicine?
- What other hobbies or activities are represented in your book that you also share an interest in? Example: Your central character is an avid knitter and so are you.
    - Do you enjoy discussing the craft of writing?
    - If you sit down with a friend, what is your favorite topic of conversation?
    - What is your background or education?
    - Are you a member of any clubs or groups?

When you are building your media empire to promote your books, whether that is writing a blog post or tweeting on Twitter, you need to find people and topics you can actively discuss with regularly. For now, start with a long list and customize it later when you get some actual readers and get a feel for what they want to hear about. The added benefit of this list is that you are also identifying like-minded people who are also likely to want to read (and buy) your book!

NOTES ON PROFESSIONS/TECHNOLOGIES/GEOGRAPHY IN YOUR ACTUAL BOOK

The reasoning for this is similar to the above—we are just trying to make sure you have plenty to discuss once you start getting yourself out there, as well as laying the groundwork for some things you might be doing later. (Hint: If your book is set in Portland, OR, there is likely to be media interest in that area).

4
WHIP YOUR WEBSITE INTO SHAPE!

Your website (www.firstnamelastname.com) is your Command Central—one centralized hub of internet "property" where people can go to read your latest blogs or articles, contact you for interviews, sign up for more information about you, and eventually buy your books. (Are you sensing a theme yet? You should be.)

If you already have your website set up and just want to skim this chapter, that's great! Here is a handy checklist so you can make sure your site doesn't have any "leaks" or places where you might be losing potential sales.

TEN ELEMENTS OF AN AUTHOR'S WEBSITE: CHECKLIST

1. **Your own domain.** This is important because you want to be sure that you own and are in control of all of your content. If your website is on a free service like Blogger, your content is retained by the site for the purpose of maintaining your account. If you haven't done it already, go over to GoDaddy (or your favorite registrar) and register your firstnamelastname.com domain.
   If someone is cybersquatting on your domain, here are some resources:
   - http://www.nolo.com/legal-encyclopedia/cybersquatting-what-what-can-be-29778.html
   - http://www.icann.org/en/help/dndr

2. **Hosting.** Next, you'll need to get hosting set up—this is the place that your website will physically "live," and does not need to be the same place where you registered the domain. You do need the "paid" hosting, because your website is your business and your property, and you will want to maintain all copyright and ownership over it. For a rundown of all your hosting options, please visit: http://bookpromotion.com/hosting

3. **Your blog.** Your site should have a blog with an RSS feed (so it stays fresh for Google and keeps your name solidly on page one of search engine results) and should be updated 2–3 times per week. It's great if

you've started a blog in a free location, but once you've established your domain/website, start blogging there instead (or at least link to your posts). You can also use syndication services like www.dlvr.it or www.ifttt.com to syndicate your blog posts so that they go out to your Facebook Fan Page, Twitter feed, or any other social media you might have. And don't worry—we will go into further detail on how to set all of these up later in the book.

4. **Photos.** Be sure to have a photo on your site so that potential readers can connect a face with your name. If you love photography and want to include it as a part of your blog or website, here are some sites you might want to check out:
    http://instagram.com
    http://flickr.com
    http://pinterest.com

5. **Email capture.** Your site should have a clear way for people to sign up to receive emails from you, whether it's an ongoing newsletter, book announcements, or updates when you post a blog entry. Give them a free chapter or report if you have to! Services for email capture include www.mailchimp.com, www.aweber.com, www.getresponse.com, or www.constantcontact.com. Be sure to put a checkbox on your "Contact Us" page for visitors to sign up for your email list. Building your list is a major element of future book sales—the more people you have on your list, the more books you can sell, and the more books you sell, the faster you get to that bestseller's list, where more people will buy your book just because you're there. Got it?

    If you are emailing your mailing list through Outlook (which gives them no way to unsubscribe), you should start integrating that list into one of these services as soon as possible so that you're in compliance with FCC regulations on emailing.

6. **Social media.** Be sure to syndicate your blog through all of your social media channels (as mentioned in # 2 above), and do a quick audit of your social media to make sure each one of your social media profiles has a link back to your main website. Make it easy for people to read your content, love it, and find their way back to your site so they can buy your books!

For a downloadable file of small social media icons, please visit http://bookpromotion.com/social.

For a complete list of social media sites, visit http://namechk.com.

7. **Your books.** Make it easy for people to buy your books once they get to your website. Include clickable bookseller logos beneath each book that go straight to the book itself on the bookseller website. For an example of this (and to download the bookseller logos), please visit http://bookpromotion.com/book. Here is an example of the "multiple bookseller logos," as applied to an actual author's website: http://www.pameladruckerman.com.

In case you're wondering, we do not recommend the words "Buy This Book Now" or "Click Here to Buy This Book," as people have a hard time figuring out that this click will actually lead them to a book. Even worse is the "Click Here to Buy This Book" with a link that just goes to a general "author's work" page on Barnes & Noble or Amazon. These things are not helping you sell books!

8. **Media.** Be sure to include links to articles you've written, as well as any radio or television interviews you've done. All of this in one place functions as an online press kit and helps to establish you as an authority in your field.

Note: If you want to develop this section further and do your own PR, we recommend Alex Carroll's publicity courses, which you can find at http://bookpromotion.com/radio. However (and this is a big however!) would not suggest doing this until you have a solid website of your own. You will definitely need a place where you can direct producers to talk about your experience, and a place to post links to radio appearances once they happen. Don't put the cart before the horse, but radio is definitely something great to consider!

9. **Contact information.** Make it easy for readers to get in touch with you (or your agent). Include a "Contact Us" form or your email address, your agent's contact info, and links to your social media. If you're on WordPress, Contact Form 7 is a great plugin for this: http://wordpress.org/extend/plugins/contact-form-7/

Also, make sure to include a place on the Contact Us form for people to opt-in to your email list. You don't necessarily have to put your email address right on your site, but you should make it as easy as possible for people to get in touch, especially if you do private consulting or speaking engagements.

10. **Analytics**. If you're not already, you should absolutely start measuring traffic to your site. Google Analytics (http://www.google.com/analytics) are an easy and free way to do this—you'll just need to sign up for an account and put the code into your website (or have your webmaster do it for you). Even if you don't want to do this, definitely call your website's hosting company and get them to point you toward your free "site stats," which they are assuredly tracking somewhere on your site.

11. **Interests.** Make sure you express your interests on your website and in your social media, even if these interests don't have anything to do with your book directly. If you love flowers, or knitting, or cars, or miniature goats, talk about that.

 You can download this whole checklist at: http://bookpromotion.com/tools-2/.

Before we move on to the next section (set up for people who have no website at all), we will stop to say, "It is totally ok if you feel overwhelmed. Take a deep breath! Rome wasn't built in a day. One step at a time. You will get there!"

WEBSITE SETUP 101

If you're just getting started, our personal preference is that you use WordPress(.org) as a content management system to set up your website. The nice thing about WordPress is that it is very easy to use and allows you to create static web pages and blog entries, as well as being extremely search engine friendly. This makes life easy as you start wanting to get fancier later on with your branding.

Here is the process for getting your website set up if you don't have one at all. We recommend that you complete these steps right away. If you already have a website or blog on a free service (like WordPress.com or Blogger), you can keep that, but you will also need to buy and build http://firstnamelastname.com so that you can take full ownership of your name and branding. You will be reading more about blogging in Chapter 7, but the answer is yes, you still need your main http://firstnamelastname.com website.

1. **Buy your URL.** Choose firstnamelastname.com or the closest approximation of this that is available. GoDaddy.com has excellent prices for URLs as well as easy-to-use hosting.

2. **Sign up for WordPress hosting**. Make sure you read the run-own on hosting companies before you sign up—there are a few security precautions you will need to put in place if you go with lower-priced hosting like GoDaddy. At this time, WPEngine is your best bet for hands-off Wordpress hosting (though, just to warn you, it does cost more).

3. **Set it up.** Once you've checked it out, follow the instructions that your hosting company sends you. If you've chosen WPEngine, they will send you an email with setup instructions.

4. **Pick a theme and upload it.** In WordPress, a theme (or template) is a pre-built design that comes with some default pieces of functionality (widgets). This is the "look and feel" of your website, and essentially takes the place of a graphic designer.

In the WordPress world, themes can either be free or paid. Either way, you want to pick a good theme. Here is our spiel on paid vs. free WordPress themes:

In WordPress, a theme (or template) is a pre-built design that comes with some default pieces of functionality (widgets). WordPress is an open-source environment, which means someone is always updating or creating something new, so this makes it easy to make your website do what you want it to do without too much hassle.

The main difference between free and fee-based themes in WordPress is that if you go with a free theme, you give up a certain amount of functionality, plus you're probably going to end up with an advertisement somewhere on your site for the company that made the theme (hey, they have to get something for making it, right?).

Here are some reasons to go with a paid theme. (Again, just our opinion. If you feel strongly about free themes, install one and get going on your site!)

FUNCTIONALITY

Paid themes tend to have good built-in SEO functionality. This becomes important when you're optimizing your site for search engines. You can get a plugin that does this (like the All-in-One SEO Pack), but then you run the risk of it conflicting with your theme. In some cases a technical conflict like this is enough to crash your whole site, and that is never a good thing. Which leads us to our next reason to go with a paid theme...

TECH SUPPORT

If you pay for a theme, you are much more likely to get the developer of that theme to help you if you have a problem. In fact, paid themes often have a robust community of users that have dealt with and solved every issue and can help you, whereas with a free theme, well, you get what you paid for. Is the developer of that free theme going to keep updating it so it keeps up with updates to the WordPress platform itself? What about testing it to keep up with plugins? Since you didn't pay for the theme, you really can't complain if the answer is no.

CUSTOMIZATION

If you pay for a theme, not only are you encouraged to customize it to meet your needs, but the developer and community that supports those themes are likely to be able to help you do so. Free themes—not so much (unless you are brave and technically oriented). With free themes you have to go into the Theme Editor and remove this code by hand. And Lori can tell you from personal, sad experience that this sometimes ends with her crashing the entire site, pounding her fist on my desk so hard it scares her dog, then starting all over by re-installing the theme from the beginning.

If you are a techie, like to learn, and don't have a tendency to pound your desk in frustration if you mess something up, start with a free theme and see how it goes! It might be just fine for your needs, and you will have saved some money.

PAID THEMES SAVE TIME

If time is a factor, definitely go with a paid theme rather than searching for and hand-installing a free theme. By the time you install a plugin for each piece of functionality you want to add, it ends up being something of a game of Jenga: Install the theme, install the plugin, activate the plugin, see if your site is still alive. Repeat ten times.

If it seems like there is a bias here toward paid themes, it's only because we (as marketers and website makers) just don't like fiddling with those free themes. If you have the time and patience and want to save money, you can absolutely start with a free theme and see how it goes.

Just so you get a feel for what themes are and how they differ, here are some examples of both free and paid themes.

Here is the gallery of free WordPress themes:
http://wordpress.org/extend/themes/

Usually there are over 1,000 themes in that gallery, all of which are free for download right now. Scroll through the gallery, pick a few themes, and download them—just so you can see how they work!

Some of the free themes we like are:
-   Bueno (a free theme offered by WooThemes.com)
-   Platform (from WordPress.com, this is the "light" version of another paid theme we like, Platform Pro)

If you know you're going to want more functionality, here are the most popular of the paid themes:
-   WooThemes.com
-   Thesis from DIYthemes.com

Once you get your theme installed and activated, next you'll start building pages. We will go along the "Author Website Checklist" from before, and let you know how to set up these elements.

1. **Your name.** Even if your URL (website address) isn't your name (like http://yourname.com), your name should still be one of the first things that users see when they go to your website so they can quickly know they're in the right place. You'll also want your name to be prominently placed so the search engines can find it and return your website in its results when people search for your name. In WordPress, you will go to Settings> General, put your name under Site Title, and replace "Just another WordPress weblog" in the tagline with something that epitomizes you or your writing.

For your convenience, we have provided a screenshot of how this should look, which you can find at:
http://www.bookpromotion.com/name

2. **Your bio.** This is a roughly 250 word summary about you—preferably a narrative about why you became a writer, something about your education if it is relevant, and a mention of some places you've been published if you already have writing credits. Go to "Pages," create a page called "About Me," and put the bio there.

For an example of this page in action, go to:
http://bookpromotion.com/aboutpage/

3. **Your picture.** As we mentioned, you want people to make the connection between your picture and your written work so they can relate to you and become your fan. You don't have to put your picture on the homepage, but you do have to put it somewhere. Add your bio to the About Me page for now.

4. **Your book.** By your book, we mean an image of your book that has images underneath it that go directly to a website where people can buy that book, like Amazon and Barnes & Noble. Basically, someone sees your writing, they see an image of the book, they click the link—it should be that easy. Make a clear and simple path for people to get your book.

To see how this works, and to download bookseller logos, go to:
http://bookpromotion.com/book.

5. **Your blog.** Whether or not you choose to write multiple blog posts (and we really encourage this for authors), you will need some examples of your writing on your website so brand-new people who

are just hearing of you can quickly get a feel for who you are and what you write about. Hopefully this sampling will make them add you to their list of favorite authors, become your fan, and buy all of your books from now on. If you do have a blog on your site, please check to make sure it has an RSS feed (usually this appears at http://firstnamelastname.com/feed). You will need this feed in order to syndicate your posts through your social media profiles.

If you are just setting up this site now, your blog will hopefully be located smack dab in the front of your site with a post that says "Welcome!," which you can feel free to replace with your own writing.

For an example of how to set up your first blog post, we've set up a screenshot for you over at:
    http://bookpromotion.com/blogpost/

6. **Press.** This is where you'll put links to interviews, articles that you write (or that are written about you), and media such as radio or TV appearances that you do. This section will be a work in progress, so don't fret about it if you don't have many media links to start—instead, use the space to put up a mini press kit about yourself, including your photo/bio, areas of expertise, and bullet points that you could discuss in an interview. Make sure your name and photo are prominently displayed, and if your name is hard to spell, make sure you sound it out. This is where producers/editors/other media people who might want to book you on shows are going to be looking, so make sure everything is super clear!

Here are a few examples of Press/Media pages on author sites:
    http://www.pameladruckerman.com/press/
    http://www.deepaprahalad.com/media-coverage/
    http://www.thebookdoctors.com/category/press

7. **Email capture.** One important component of your website is going to be a capture form for people to enter their email addresses. In case we haven't already made this clear enough, you are building up

your audience of readers, and part of doing that is keeping in touch with them regularly.

Whether you'd prefer to have subscribers be automatically emailed when you post a blog or you'd like to manually send them an update or newsletter every month, we recommend MailChimp.com to store your email list. They have a great set of features, your account is free up to 2,000 subscribers, and their site is clear and easy to use. Mailchimp for the win!

Other email capture services include Aweber, Constant Contact, and GetResponse. These services are paid, and many of them have similar RSS-to-Email services. Check out all of them before you sign up—once you start building a list, it is not easy (at all) to move your list over to another service.

Once you sign up for the service of your preference and create a capture code for people's email addresses, put that code into one of the "Text" widgets in the "Appearance" section of your website.

To see a screen shot of the Appearance> Widget section and the text box where you put the code, visit:
http://bookpromotion.com/textbox

8. **Contact information.** You'll definitely need links to your social media profiles, preferably somewhere on the homepage so interested reporters, publishers, and other people who might want to help you with your career can find and connect you. You don't necessarily have to put your email address right on your site (for instance, you might want to use a Contact Us form), but you should make it as easy as possible for people to get in touch, especially if you do private consulting or speaking engagements. If you want to use a Contact Us form, we would recommend a plugin called Contact Form 7.

9. **Analytics.** You need to be able to track how many people are going to your site, where they're coming from, and how long they're staying, so you can take the appropriate action to get these numbers to be where you want them. You'll need a Google account for this as well, so pull out your information and log in to http://google.com/analytics. You will go through a series of steps to register your site, then you'll be given a short block of code to copy. The simplest way to get that

code into your site is to download a plugin (from within the WordPress dashboard) called "Google Analytics for WordPress" and activate it while you're logged in to your Google Analytics account. That way, you can connect the accounts and start seeing your statistics when you log in to your website.

10. **Syndication.** Once you start posting on your blog, you'll want those blog posts to go out to your Twitter feed, your Facebook profile/page, and any other social media accounts you open. You can do this manually during your daily "social media time," or if you're a little more tech-savvy and brave, you can also open a free account at HootSuite (http://hootsuite.com). HootSuite will allow you to pull the RSS feed from your blog and distribute it to various social media outlets like Facebook and Twitter. You can also pre-schedule tweets and status updates AND monitor your mentions in the world of social media. Handy! If you're not a HootSuite fan, that's fine—try www.twitterfeed.com or www.ifttt.com

11. **Your book trailer (if you have one).** Book trailers have been around a long time, and were originally used as part of the advance package sent along to bookstores and reviewers. Because book tours were done in person, the bookstore liked to have a way of knowing what the event (in particular the author's appearance and presence) would look like. A lot has changed since that first usage, and they are popping up all over the place these days, especially by indie authors trying to differentiate themselves from mainstream authors. We're not going to go into huge detail on the book trailer here, because we're trying to get you through the setup process and out promoting that book. But if this is something you've already got, be sure to include it on your site.

NEW TOPIC: GOOGLE AUTHORSHIP!

So much can happen in a year! Since the first edition of this book came out, Google introduced a very important concept called "Authorship." As you can see, if you've set up your Google Authorship correctly by linking your written stuff that's online with your Google + profile, your photo will appear next to things you've written. This is handy, not just for search engine purposes, but because it will make people click on your stuff more readily since they will know it's by you and associate the content with your brand (your brand being your little face).

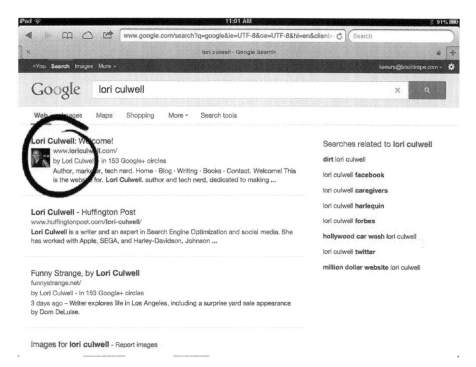

Google Authorship definitely makes the click through rate for your written work go up. However, it does take awhile to get approved, so you should go over and apply to have your Authorship verified right away.

To apply for your own Google Authorship status, go to:

http://plus.google.com/authorship

(you will need that Gmail/Google Plus account again, so keep it handy!)

5
SET UP SOCIAL MEDIA PROFILES

OK, you've gotten everything set up, all digital roads lead back to you, and your Google Page One results will make us proud, right?

You probably know about the major social media profiles, even if you're not using them already. So, which ones do you actually need to use, and when? This will depend largely on preference, as you're more likely to stick with something you actually like, but as a general rule, the answer is to establish your presence on all of them. To give you an idea of how quickly things move here in internet land, when we first wrote this book, we talked about the "big three". Now clearly, there are more than just these out there, and in fact, we will talk about a few more of them. But, if you want to really hit the primary sources, these are the must-haves. Think of the "big five" social media platforms this way:

- **Twitter** – A cocktail party
- **Facebook** – A family reunion/neighborhood block party
- **Google Plus** – A conversation amongst friends and acquaintances.
- **Pinterest** – A scrapbooking party or bulletin board in a local coffee shop.
- **LinkedIn** – A business conference

Let's get you set up on each one so you can start interacting. Open up that folder full of research/profile information/photos of yourself, and get ready to sign up!

TWITTER

We know, we know! The moment you saw the title, you rolled your eyes. You have some preconceived notions about Twitter, perhaps, and you just don't even know where to start.

Now's the time for a little bit of tough love. Twitter, in case you didn't know, is a hugely popular social media platform with more than 500 million users (and counting). Twitter is really important for writers especially, because it is a FREE way of talking back and forth with people, which eventually will get you more followers and readers.

Side note: If you're a Twitter user already, great! Our work here is (partially) done. Just to make sure you're using Twitter to its optimal advantage, please jump ahead to the "How to Use Twitter" section in Part Two and check everything off while we're getting everyone else up to speed.

Second side note: If you're a Facebook user (meaning, you have a Facebook Fan Page for yourself or one or more of your books), but you haven't made the jump over to Twitter yet, we cannot recommend strongly enough that you go over and open up a Twitter account, just to get used to using both platforms. The reason for this is simple: It is not easy to meet new people on Facebook, or get new fans, or spread the word about your work without a monetary investment. Here's why. Facebook makes its money by selling Facebook Ads, and their system is set up to make it almost impossible to grow a huge network of followers unless you take out a Facebook ad to drive people over to that page. Facebook limits the amount of friends you can have on a personal profile (5,000 is the max), plus they also recommend that you NOT friend people that you don't actually know (like friends of friends), specifically because once you use their platform for this kind of business expansion and networking, you are promoting a business or a product, and this violates their terms of service. Facebook makes it clear: If you are promoting something (like a book) to people you don't know, you need to do that through your Facebook Fan Page (and an ad). Simple, right?

Totally simple—if you have name recognition or a famous book already, OR you have a large budget to build up your fan base through ads. Not so simple if what you have more of is time and energy to put toward your own promotion.

So—back to Twitter. Unlike Facebook, there is no reason why you can't engage people you don't know by chatting with them on Twitter. By having a link in your profile, you will then drive them over to your website. In fact, once you get a reputation on Twitter for being an expert in something, you will start seeing an increase in traffic anyway, because the smarter you are, the more people want to know about you.

Again, this is not applicable to you if you have a huge budget to advertise and build your fan base, but if you do not have this, Twitter is by far the most economical and effective form of lead generation for finding new fans. So without further delay, let's get you started!

TWITTER SETUP INSTRUCTIONS:

1. Go to http://twitter.com and log in if you already have an account. If you don't, click the Sign Up button and follow the simple instructions to create an account.

2. Go to your email and click the link that Twitter will send you to authenticate/verify your account.

3. Go to the Profile section under Settings, upload a photo, and fill in all the information (see, your Bio information and photo are already coming in handy!). Just so you don't get stuck and frustrated, the profile photo for Twitter needs to be approximately 73 pixels by 73 pixels. Don't ask us why—it's just what works best.

Here is a screenshot of Lori's Twitter Profile Page, for your reference:

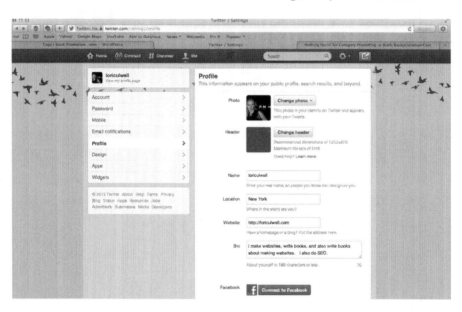

If you are still feeling ambitious after all of this, you can feel free to go over to the Design tab and change your background to something less generic than the Twitter default, but DO NOT WORRY about making your Twitter background/website/Facebook all look the same right this minute. We would much rather have you get in there and start having some actual conversations, rather than waiting until everything is "perfect." Just get in there and get started!

FACEBOOK

Facebook is a destination site—meaning people go there to participate in an online conversation. It is a more passive medium than some social networking sites (such as Twitter). People are therefore predisposed to be curious about postings, and information can live there indefinitely once it's posted. While primarily geared towards connecting people to people, it has increasingly become popular in connecting people with topics, companies, and products.

If you are already on Facebook to communicate with your friends—great! Then you already know how to use the platform, so it's one less thing you will need to learn. Whether or not you have a personal Facebook page, you'll want to start up a Facebook Fan Page for yourself as an author. Here you can make announcements about your book(s), communicate with your fans (without having to personally accept all of their friend requests), and give those fans a chance to share your work with their friends.

In case you're not familiar with the difference between a profile on Facebook and a Fan Page, here is a basic overview:

In a Facebook Profile:

- "Friend requests" are sent to and received by friends, family, friends of friends, etc.
- Personal information is shared on your "wall" for your friends to see/comment on.
- You can comment on other people's photos, "like" their posts, play games, and do other fun Facebook things.
- You may mention your books, but if you do it so much that you cross the line into "marketing," Facebook has the right to ban you

On a Facebook Fan Page:

- Your fans only need to "Like" the page to gain access.
- You may market on the page to your heart's content.
- Other people may be administrators of the page to make updates when you're not around.
- You may include information about all of your books, a feed from your blog, and a link out to your website.
- Your updates will appear in the feed of all those who have "Liked" the page.

Hopefully this makes things a little more clear. You will need to have both a Facebook profile AND a Facebook Fan Page, because in order to use all of the functionality that Facebook has to offer, you need to first log in as a PERSON WITH A PROFILE, then create and be the administrator of a page.

You are probably wondering, "Why would I need both? That seems confusing and unnecessary. I should just be able to create a Facebook account and use it on my own behalf to market my brand/sell my books."

Yes, you are right in thinking that way, and Facebook is going in that direction (if you are the Nike Corporation, you probably have that kind of access). For now, though, it SIMPLY WORKS BETTER if you have at least one profile connected to the page. Another option is to create a profile, leave it empty, and then make the page. Or simply have someone with a Facebook account make the page for you.

Here are some examples of some Facebook Fan Pages for authors:

http://facebook.com/DavidSedaris

http://facebook.com/JamesPatterson01

http://facebook.com/Pamela.Druckerman

Facebook Fan Page setup instructions:

First, go to Facebook (http://facebook.com) and log in as yourself. If you don't have an account, just go ahead and open one as a regular person (NOT AS THE NAME OF YOUR BOOK). Go through the verification process.

Next, go to http://www.facebook.com/pages/create.php.

The page should look like this:

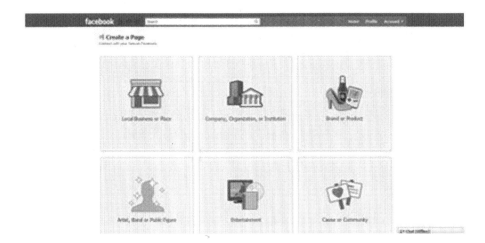

If you are making a page for one specific book, choose the Brand or Product option. If you are making a page for yourself as an author, choose the Artist, Band, or Public Figure option.

Assuming that you've chosen the Artist, Band, or Public Figure option, choose Author in the drop-down menu and then put your name in the box beneath it. After reading and agreeing to the terms of service (which reiterates the fact that you either ARE this person or are authorized to act on their behalf), click "Get Started."

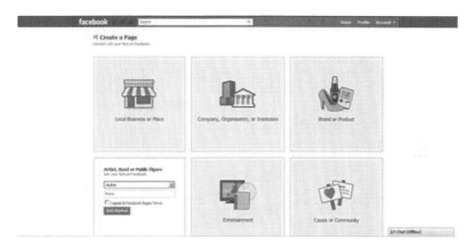

Voila! Author Fan Page. Next you will just need to add things like your photo (aren't you glad you have a few of those in that folder on your desktop?), a photo of your book cover (again, thank goodness for that folder!), and some information about you (AGAIN, wow, so glad we did all that preparation work on your biography, a summary of your book, and a look at your website).

Next, you can simply go over to http://facebook.com/username, select the page you want to rename, and change the username of your Fan Page to your own name. You can't change the name, so be sure to pick a name you like!

Changing your Facebook username is a simple and no-cost way to improve the search engine ranking for your name.

If you already changed the username of your Facebook Profile to your name, that's fine. Just use the word "Author" before or after your name for the Fan Page. That would look like this:

http://facebook.com/AuthorFirstNameLastName

Again, don't let any of this bog you down. You are going for the quickest and most organized set up possible so that your fans can consume your content on the platform where they feel most comfortable. You don't have to become a social media expert. As long as you have something that has your name on it and links over to your website where people can buy your books, let's move on.

GOOGLE+ (PLUS.GOOGLE.COM/)

The primary feature of Google+ is the use of circles. Essentially you add people to various circles, which you create. We think the best thing about this is that you can create circles called things like "business acquaintances" or "other book pros." For those of us who have been combining personal interests with business on Facebook for years, this is a neat trick.

You can find Google Plus at http://plus.google.com/. You will need a gmail account to create your Google Plus Page (you should have a gmail account anyway for all the other useful tools like Google Analytics, etc, so if you don't have one, that's the place to start. http://gmail.com

The other feature we like is the ability to "hang out" with people without adding them to your circles. In other words, they become an associate only as long as you are hanging out with them, and then you can add them or not.

Every time Facebook makes another huge change, more people adopt Google+, so it's definitely worth adding it to your network, just so you can reach the maximum amount of people.

PINTEREST (PINTEREST.COM)

Talk about speed of light growth! Pinterest was barely a blip on the radar in our first version of this book, and it has taken the social media world by storm. If you think about the name of the site, you can see that it stands for what it is – the ability to "pin things of interest" and that is very descriptive of what you do, and how you do it. The good news is, of all the social media sites, most people find this the simplest to use. The bad news is, it is still too soon to tell whether the platform is well suited to authors actually selling books. It is certainly an excellent discoverability tool, and because of the highly visual nature of the medium, most people find it quite satisfying.

Just like the other options listed here, step one is to head on over to Pinterest and set up your profile. You have the option of using your Facebook or Twitter account (which you have just set-up, as you recall) or you can create a brand new account tied to an email address. The only benefit to using an existing account is that you will be able to find and follow your existing friends more easily that way. Aside from that, there isn't much difference one way or the other. Head on over to http://pinterest.com/ and get signed up.

We strongly recommend that you also download the "Pin it" button for your browser. This allows you to pin anything you like as you are surfing the web. This makes it easy to add things of interest as you go about your day online, with very minimal effort. We will talk about what you might pin, and why later on. For now, just download the add-on for your browser here http://about.pinterest.com/goodies/ .

LINKEDIN (LINKEDIN.COM/)

Pinterest also has apps for your phone, or iPad, etc. Once you are signed up, all the various versions will synch together, no matter which one you are using. We'll discuss what you do once you are on there in the later sections of the book.

LinkedIn will not be appropriate for all books, however it may be for those that are business related. This will work best if you are available and willing to participate in LinkedIn Groups as a subject matter expert.

For now, just go over to http://linkedin.com, sign up for an account, and go through the verification process. Take the same bio information, photo, and the link to your website, and fill out the profile on LinkedIn. Be sure to change your profile name so that it is your actual Firstname/Lastname, which you can do by logging in to Linked In, then going to the Profile tab, then clicking Edit Profile.

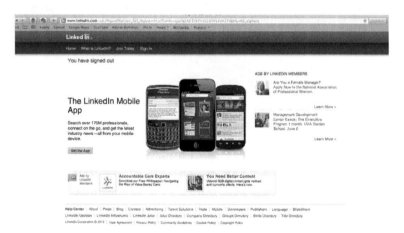

Now that we've got the basic setup covered, let's get you out in the world, connecting with people and building up your readership. After all, that's why we're here, right?

6
GET ON THE BOOK SITES

There are several key book sites in which you might want to participate. At the bare minimum, you will want to at least update your information on Amazon to make it easier for potential readers to find you.

- Amazon.com—As we might have mentioned, Amazon.com is the 5th most popular website in the world, and has more than 5 million books on its site at any given time.

- BN.com—This is the online version of book retailing giant Barnes & Noble. They have less power in the online world, but this is still an area where you want to stay up to date. (Note: Having your book on their website has absolutely nothing to do with getting it into their retail stores.)

- Goodreads.com—Unlike the two sites above, Goodreads does not sell books. You can think of them as a gathering place for book lovers, or as an enormous online book club. As of March 2013 Goodreads has been acquired by Amazon. The plan as announced, indicates that they intend to operate it as an independent entity (i.e. few changes) but it is truly too soon to tell. Check www.bookpromotion.com for the latest news!

- LibraryThing.com—Like Goodreads, this site is not a book seller. It was originally started as a way for people to keep track of their books and share lists of favorites with other readers. It has become quite a meeting place for readers, and so it can be a good way to generate discussions about you and your book.

- Shelfari.com—Shelfari was officially launched in October 2006 and was acquired by Amazon.com in August 2008. It is essentially a competitor to Goodreads, but with a better tie-in to Amazon. Despite that big name support, it is not nearly as popular as Goodreads or LibraryThing. Still, it is best not to ignore it, as one never knows where your best supporters will come from.

AMAZON.COM

Amazon.com has tens of millions of users visiting them every day. Simply put, you must have a presence there.

Author Central

Author Central is available to any published author, whether it's one short story on Kindle or multiple novels. Please note that you cannot create a login here until you have books for sale on Amazon.com.

Go to Author Central and create a login:
https://authorcentral.amazon.com/

You will use your customer account login first, so they can associate the two. If you do not have a customer login for Amazon.com, then you will need to create one. Once you have successfully logged in, you will see this:

As you can see, they make it very easy for you to add what you need to your profile. Take care of getting your profile established before you dive into any of those other tempting tabs (the Sales tab being the most tempting of all).

- Update your profile. In your profile you can (and should) have: a biography, a photo, a link to your website and to your Twitter stream, a list of upcoming events you will be attending or in which you will be participating (keep this current!), and uploaded videos you may have of yourself that pertain to your book. View or edit your list of books (surprisingly this is often inaccurate).

- Add your blog. If you have taken our advice, you have one of these and should add it here!

- Search Inside the Book. Some authors are nervous about this because it requires you to upload your entire manuscript (most publishers participate in this as a regular policy). It then shows interested browsers selections from your book. But they do it randomly, with different selections each click. Do you know how long it would take someone to compile your entire book? We don't either, but it would take quite some time! If they go to that level of trouble, they are clearly huge fans and you should feel good about that. The real reason you WANT your book to have this feature is that it allows Amazon to apply a search algorithm to your book, which will help people doing relevant keyword searches to find it. If you do not use Search Inside the Book, the keyword searches will solely be based on the short description provided.

Now that you have your critical information on Amazon and are a much more legitimate-looking author, let's talk a bit more about what other information you can find in Author Central.

Sales Info

This is one area that could stand some improvement, so it would not be surprising to see an update coming soon. The sales information shown here only includes data from Book Scan. Book Scan is the service most publishers and other industry professionals use to track book sales. It is usually fee-based, and is based on barcode scans. So, any books sold anywhere, theoretically, should be represented here. We say theoretically because it depends on many factors, not the least of which is that the bookseller has to actually use a barcode scanner system and have it linked in to the system. It also has a bit of a time lag (we have actually watched orders go through in the publishing system that show up days later).

The other fatal flaw in the system (in our opinion), is that it currently represents only your physical book sales, and does not even take into account your Kindle sales at this stage. If you are self-published, you can obviously log in to the Kindle Digital Publishing area and check your sales as often as you like. For those of you who have gone the traditional route, you are reliant on your publisher for that information.

Lastly, it seems unlikely that you will ever see sales from the other e-book sellers (Apple, Smashwords, Barnes & Noble, etc.) so this data is merely going to give you one slice of your actual earnings pie. But this is better than nothing.

Customer Reviews

This area consolidates all the reviews you have for all of your books. Do not linger here too long—this can be a slippery slope. We know it is tempting to check this constantly, eagerly awaiting the glowing reviews! We do it for the books we work on, of course. But be aware that you cannot avoid getting a negative review forever. Not every book is for every reader; that is just a fact. The point of reviews is to help others decide whether they will like your book. So really, if a negative review helps someone avoid it who will actually not like it, you are better off. And let's be honest, some people are jerks and just think it is fun to leave negative reviews!

Here is another important concern with customer reviews. When looking at your reviews, it's important to be mentally prepared so you don't get emotional and start arguing with the reviewers. You might (no, you will) be tempted to respond to the negative reviews. It is human nature to defend one's young, and your book is your baby. DON'T do it! It is unprofessional, and will not change the review in any way. Try your hardest to chalk it up to part of life as an author, and shrug it off. If by some odd chance the review has some actually useful feedback, take it on advisement for your next book, but still move on and do not engage the reviewer.

**Exception to the rule—a note to the self-published folks: If you are using e-book–only formats, or print on demand, you can update your book at virtually any time, for little to no cost. As a result, if you see several reviews mentioning a functional issue with your book (typos, additional characters added, missing pages, etc.) you can and should address those issues. BUT do not be surprised if even after fixing them, you see reviews with similar content. For some reason, once people see that there is an "issue," they are predisposed to see it themselves, whether it continues to be an issue or not. So, after you are sure you have the problem licked, go back to shrugging off the not-so-great reviews.

Amazon Author Rank

This is a feature introduced in October 2012. According to Amazon this is "the definitive list of best-selling authors on Amazon.com. This list makes it easy for readers to discover the best-selling authors on Amazon.com overall and within a selection of major genres.

Amazon Author Rank is your rank based on the sales of all of your books on Amazon.com. Just like Amazon Best Sellers, it is updated hourly. The top 100 authors overall and the top 100 in selected genres will be displayed on Amazon.com. You can see your Amazon Author Rank trended over time in Author Central.

You can find your Amazon Author Rank in Author Central under the Rank tab. Historical ranking data is available from September 28, 2012." At present it is still unclear how this is being used. We include it here, although we can't say there is much you can do about it, or with it, aside from doing your best to market (and therefore sell) more books.

What else to do on Amazon?

Your book is going to be pulled in automatically once it is available in a catalogue, via its ISBN number. The data that shows there is mostly auto-generated based on how your publisher input it into the system. If something is inaccurate, you can submit a form which will ask for a correction, but this is limited to specific quantifiable things like edition number and page count. Anything else is managed by the publisher.

**Self-published authors: There are actually many things that can be done at the submission stage, but since there is plenty of really great information available in the help forums, we will not address them here. If you do nothing else, be sure your BISAC codes are accurately set up, as those are what will identify your categories in Amazon.

GOODREADS, LIBRARYTHING, AND SHELFARI

You are probably wondering why we have lumped these all together. The answer is that basically you need to do almost exactly what you just did for Amazon on those sites as well. Nearly everything we just outlined for you above also applies to these sites. They all have logins, profiles, reviewers, even lists. Here are a couple of unique features that you will want to be aware of, but overall your goal is to go to each one and create your profile the same way you have everywhere else.

Goodreads (goodreads.com)

This is truly a social networking platform for readers. As we mentioned previously, it has very recently (March 2013) been acquired by Amazon, and it is not clear what impact that will have. We can assume the basic structure will remain the same. As with most social networks, you can friend people, message them, and generally communicate. Also, as with all social networks, the more active you are, the more you get out of it. You will need to decide for yourself how far you want to pursue your participation. There are some things that we would say are in your "mandatory" category, however:

1. Create your profile and claim your author page. Unlike Amazon where you are the default owner, Goodreads and the librarians are the owners of any page not claimed. It is a simple process: Find your name, then click on the link that says, "Are you the author of this book?" Once you have claimed it, you are labeled a "Goodreads Author," and only you have control over your page.

2. If you are inclined to use this site, it will be worth your time to put some books onto your "shelves." Shelves are divided into "to read," "reading," and "read." It is always good to have your book on peoples' shelves, so reciprocate the favor ahead of time by doing the same. Also, once you have 50 books on your shelves, you can apply to be a Librarian, which gives you some added things you can do, like edit book listings and consolidate your titles (Kindle and print frequently show up as separate listings).

So go on over and start up a profile!

LibraryThing (librarything.com)

LibraryThing is similar to Goodreads in its purpose—it is a community of readers who like to interact about books. It originally started as an online "card catalogue" to keep track of books that avid readers had read. As to functionality, you also add books you have read, but with the additional feature that then people will recommend additional books to you based on what you have read. Another key difference with LibraryThing is that you can upgrade your LibraryThing membership for a fee. The fee is solely so that you can catalogue more books. It is cheap, but aside from the quantity of books you can list as yours, we don't see any valuable features associated with the membership. Signing up is so simple that there is no need to include a screen shot. Here is a link to their relevant help text on the topic of claiming your author status:

http://www.librarything.com/about_authors.php

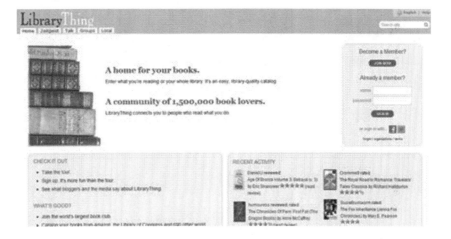

Shelfari (shelfari.com)

The good news about Shelfari is that because it is linked to Amazon, you don't need to create a new login. You can also import your purchased books from Amazon, so it is far easier to populate your shelves. Readers interact and discuss books in the same way as on the previously mentioned sites. So far this is not the leader in the space, nor does it seem to be as integrated into Amazon as had been expected when they were acquired. Still, as with all the seeds we are telling you to plant, it is best to at least create a basic profile and put all your usual information and links into it.

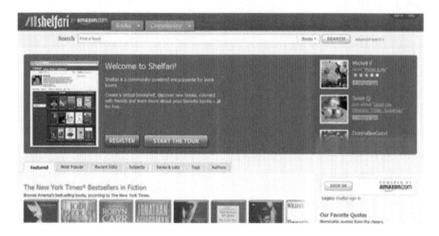

BARNES & NOBLE (BN.COM)

BN.com is their online presence. You may be wondering why we didn't put this up under Amazon.com, as on the surface they would be equivalent. Unfortunately, that is not the case. At the time of this writing, you have little to no ability to control what is on BN.com about your book. And you don't have to worry about your author information, because at the moment there is none. If you click on the name of an author on their site, it merely brings up a search on the author's name.

Here is an excerpt from their FAQs:

> For Data Corrections
> If you have any product page corrections, please email them to
> corrections@barnesandnoble.com.

Include the ISBN in all your correspondence, and be specific about the changes that need to be made. Please include your name and contact number for verification purposes.

If you would like to add content, such as a "From the Publisher" description or cover images to the product page, please send them to *titles@bn.com*.

So, your only job is to check to see if the listing is accurate, and then leave it alone. A few reviews here wouldn't hurt and you can feel free to encourage friends, family, and book bloggers to post to the Barnes & Noble site as well, but it is secondary by far to the other sites even in that regard.

THE BIG PICTURE: AUTHOR PLATFORM FOR REPUTATION MANAGEMENT

By now you might be wondering—why, exactly, would I need to set up ALL of these different accounts, when there is no way one person could ever use all of them?

This is actually a valid question, and I (Lori) am going to put on my SEO (Search Engine Optimization) expert hat for a moment to explain why a website based on your own name as well as exposure across multiple platforms (if only for syndication and reputation management purposes) is something you definitely need. In fact, I want you to pay attention to this so much, I have employed Internet Marketing Related Stock Photography (above). Hey look! A graphic! Pay attention!

First off, what exactly is "Reputation Management," and why on earth would you care about a thing like this? You're just minding your own business and writing awesome books, which is how it should be. Steven Pressfield is right when he says (in "The War of Art") that spending too much time on social media is a distraction and an excuse.

However (and this is a big however), establishing yourself on the various social sites is important, and here is why:

When someone "Googles" you, all roads on Page One of search results for your name should lead directly to you, and setting up your social media properly is one way to insure that happens. Page One of Google results for your name should belong to you and only you, and should offer only opportunities for you to sell books (or soap, or your hair salon, or just your good name-- whatever you happen to be putting out there in the world right now). Page One of Google is not where you want a mention of say, the fact that someone doesn't like you, or a bad review of one of your books (or your business), or anything that might get in the way of the good impression you're trying to make.

Just for fun, let's take a look at the results I get when I Google Michael Pollan, the author of "Omnivore's Dilemma." I like Michael's website and think he's savvy when it comes to social media and generally being organized, so I'm confident his Google results will be a great example.

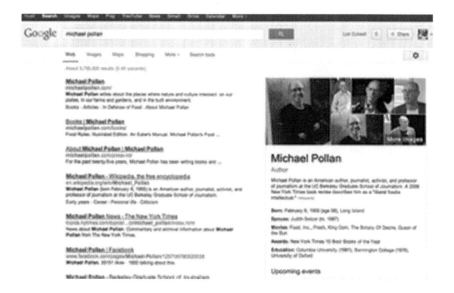

Here we go! As you can see, Michael has a website based on his own name, so Google is of course showing pages from his site as the first three results when you Google him. This is excellent news for him, and means that anyone that searches for him is likely to quickly find their way to his excellent website, where they will find examples of his writing and be given opportunities to sign up for his newsletter, buy his books, and follow him on their preferred form of social media. The next entry down is a Wikipedia page, which is great to have, but which needs to come about organically (meaning, it is frowned upon to make a Wikipedia page for yourself). If you keep producing excellent work, eventually your Wikipedia page will happen. Let's move on to the next result down: the Amazon Author Central listing. Amazon Author Central is definitely something you can control, and if you have books out, you should go over there and flesh your Author Central listing out so it appears in Google.

https://authorcentral.amazon.com/gp/home

Next result down: Michael's Twitter account. You'll notice that he's not even that much of an active "back and forth" tweeter, using his Twitter stream mainly to syndicate his articles. This is a perfectly acceptable use of Twitter if the medium just doesn't appeal to you. Notice that his Twitter page ranks in Google, his profile contains a link back to his main website, and (as I mentioned), his feed is being used mainly for syndication, so there is always fresh content going through there. Another example of "all roads lead back to the author."

Other results (not shown here because they fell below what I could capture in a screenshot): Pollan's Facebook Fan Page, which also syndicates his content, and his GoodReads profile, which is also filled out, contains a photo, and has a link back to his main website. He teaches at the Berkeley School of Journalism and writes for the New York Times, so those profile pages are also included.

If you're about to say, "I don't write for the New York Times, so how do I get a link like that?" I will simply encourage you to volunteer to write for publications and blogs/websites with more traffic than your own to obtain this kind of listing.

In case you're wondering, what you're doing here is traditional SEO (search engine optimization), using your name as the primary keyword for which you're optimizing. This should be a relatively simple feat to accomplish, given the fact that there is likely low competition for your name because you're not famous (yet).

Also, don't assume that you'll just wait until your work becomes well known, and then your Page One results will magically fix themselves. This is not true, and in fact, I have been hired several times by famous authors to undo the damage this nonchalance has caused. In one instance, a famous author wrote a controversial article years ago, and was now releasing a parenting book. She (and her publishers) just wanted people to give her new book a chance if/when they Googled her, and this was less likely with that controversial article all over her Page One results. It took more than a year, but I can now say that when you Google her, you don't get to the controversy until Page Three (in SEO terms, we call this "where they bury bodies").

I have also been hired by a famous author with a more common name, just to "clean up" his Google presence, which in his case just meant making sure that Page One results didn't show several not-so-nice articles written about him and one of his books. In this case (as well as the other one, above), if this author had been more diligent about his web presence, he wouldn't have needed me in the first place.

PART TWO: GET YOURSELF OUT THERE!

Now that you've got your "hub" website and all of your social media organized and in place, the next step is to go out there in the internet world to draw interested people in, which will build up your following and help you sell books. You'll need to put some time aside every day into making connections, getting out there, and just being visible so that people see what you have to offer.

Here's the great news: You're already an expert in your field AND you have all of your assets organized, so all that's left is to point you in the right direction. We're just going to give you the tools and places to share your knowledge.

7
BLOGGING/NETWORKING

Now that we've gotten you a bit more organized, let's talk about why you would use one or more of these tools to begin your marketing efforts. Some things we discuss are necessary no matter what your platform and book topic, and others are more specialized. We will help you narrow down which things you should do and how to prioritize your activities. The internet is a vast and constantly evolving place, so while we will do our best to be comprehensive you will need to keep your eyes and ears open for new opportunities you can leverage.

GENERAL "NETIQUETTE"

There are many nuances of site-specific etiquette that we will attempt to outline in the related sections, but here are some general things to be aware of:

-   You need to use ethical standards in your communications. The internet has a very long memory, so if you fabricate information or data, someone, somewhere, will find out. Just don't go there.

-   For specifics, the Word of Mouth Marketing Association (WOMMA) http://www.womma.org/ has fantastic guidelines and does regular research on what most internet sites consider standard ethical guidelines.

-   Do not just "sell." You need to engage in an ongoing online conversation. Would you continue to converse with someone who said, "Buy my book" in response to everything you said? Probably not. If you create a meaningful online presence, your book will be mentioned passively on a routine basis (remember all those signatures you created in step one?).
-   When in doubt, ask. Most online communities will post frequently asked questions (FAQs) and behavioral guidelines. If you do not see what you need, and are in doubt as to procedure, you should simply

communicate with a moderator, a site contact, or more experienced member, explaining that you are new and have a question. Everyone was new once, and you will find that responses are helpful and generally welcoming. **Note:** It would be generous of you to keep your eye out later to offer similar help as other new people come along.

- Be a person, but not too personal. You will need to decide for yourself how much information is too much. You will also need to decide how open you want to be about your family life, and whether that is relevant to your platform. If you have written a book about motherhood, you probably will have to divulge some details of your own life with respect to that, for example.

- Religion and politics. We were tempted just to leave the bullet point at that. No topics are as fraught with peril as religion and politics. As with personal information, you need to decide whether this is relevant to your readership, and/or whether you are going to alienate a demographic you want to buy your book by being too forthcoming about your views.

- Do not be a troll. A troll in internet lingo is someone who is deliberately negative with the intent of provoking a response. This phenomenon is unfortunately quite prevalent and it is inevitable that you will encounter one eventually. As long as you endeavor not to be one yourself, you can at least know you are helping make the internet a better place.

THINK I'M GONNA BLOG

One of the reasons we had you explore your interests in Chapter 3 was to give you some idea of what you might want to say in your blog. Now is the time! You're going to start blogging 1–3 times per week.

Here is the most important thing to know about your blog: Its sole purpose is to attract readers, who will also become readers of your book. So whatever you write about, whatever you post, ask yourself the simple question, "Who are my readers, and what do they like to read?"

Tips:

- Don't feel each blog entry needs to be a 500–1,000 word mini-novel. A paragraph is fine. A sentence is fine. A photo with a caption is fine. Blogging regularly is more important than crafting the blog equivalent of a Pulitzer Prize winning article.

- You don't even have to write each entry yourself! You can ask other bloggers you like (we will talk about them in a minute) to write a guest post for you. As long as they are topically relevant to your blog, your readers will appreciate the variety a guest blog post can bring.

- On occasion it is ok to discuss your book, as long as it is not a constant plea for purchase. When you get your cover image for the first time, posting it on your blog would be totally appropriate. And it is expected that you will post links to any other blogs that mention you or your book, so touting those awesome reviews from other bloggers is also considered good form.

- Blog about what inspires you, what bothers you, or what moves you. But do it in a way that is amusing or enlightening for your readers. If you have a reason to include your personal life in your blog (if, say, you know your readers are working mothers like you) then be sure you post material that is appropriate to that audience. Remember, what you put out there will likely live out there forever, so think about it before you post it—but *do post it!*

We know you love writing, so it's going to be no problem to blog it up, right? Just in case you run out of time/things to say, here are some other tools you can use to help you produce content on a regular basis to keep your readers entertained.

PHOTO SHARING

Photo sharing allows you to share photos online (publically or privately) by publishing them through websites and applications that let users upload and display images. It also provides permanent and centralized access to photos. Utilizing photo-sharing sites is a great way to connect with your readers visually and provide accounts of promotional events and other photo ops related to your book release.

Flickr (flickr.com)

Flickr is one of the most popular online photo management and sharing applications where users can keep a blog of photos or share photo collections publicly and privately. Photos can be loaded into the system from the web, mobile devices, computers, and other software and shared via the Flickr website in RSS feeds, by email, and by posting to outside blogs. Use this service to upload your photos from a book tour, of you speaking at an event, or of you just holding up your book—whatever works!

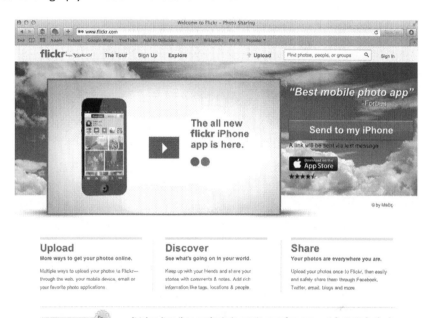

TwitPic (twitpic.com)

TwitPic lets you post photos or videos to TwitPic from your phone, from the site, or through email and then use those photos in your tweets on Twitter. All you need is your username and password from Twitter.

Many things about this service are catered specifically to Twitter—TwitPic URLs are short, so you don't have to use URL shortening services to include your photo in a post. Comments to photographs are then sent as a reply tweet. So TwitPic can be best used as a way to make your tweets richer and more interesting by including a photo, but it can also be used independently of Twitter, similar to Flickr.

There are several other photo sharing services that can be used to upload photos to Twitter, including applications specifically created for iPhones, BlackBerry, and Android phones.

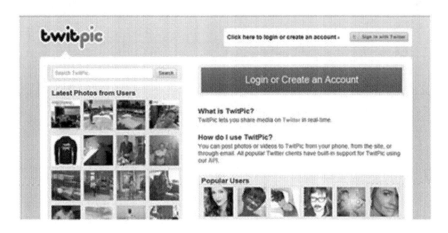

Instagram (instagr.am)

Instagram is a free photo sharing service that allows you to choose a filter to transform the look of your photos, post directly to Instagram, and even share them with your Facebook, Twitter, and Tumblr networks. Invented to be a sort of hybrid between the Polaroid cameras and telegrams of yore, Instagram is intended to be a sort of "magical" way to share your life with family and friends through a series of photos.

What makes Instagram special is the treatment that photos get through the 11 available filters, which allow photos to look more professional, the ability to share on multiple networks at once, and an easy, optimized uploading experience. Photos are shared with anyone who uses Instagram, unless you opt in to a private option in which the user approves all follow requests.

The first Instagram platform was created for iPhone (available for free in the iTunes app store), but according to their website, more platforms are on the way soon. Current networks available for sharing through Instagram include Flickr, Facebook, Twitter, and Foursquare. And just like the plan for platform expansion, more networks are planned to be added in the future.

TOOLS FOR MEETUPS/LIVE BROADCAST

Justin.tv (justin.tv)

Justin.tv is a website which consists of a network of diverse channels providing a platform for video streaming events online. For writers, it is especially useful for live-streaming events such as book readings. Whatever show you choose to create, during your broadcast on Justin.tv viewers can communicate back to you (and talk to each other) via an optional chat room and also leave comments and rate your show. This feature can be a great asset for writers to connect with their reading community because it lets you get instant feedback from your audience and field questions in real time. By recording your show you can also make it available for viewing later.

Justin.tv also offers a paid service level for $9.99 a month, which has additional features and allows you to view and use the service advertisement free. If this is really your thing, and you intend to provide regular quality content, you can also consider applying for Producer status. Producer content is highlighted on the site, and promoted much more extensively, so this could be worthwhile if you find the service is to your liking.

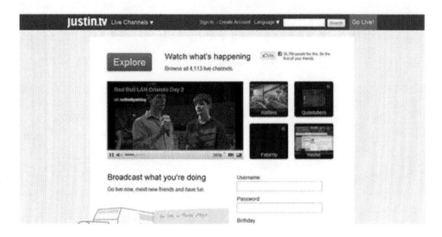

Google Plus Hangouts

Google Plus Hangouts are easy, fast ways to virtually connect with others around the globe. Chats can be public or private allowing you to utilize it for anything from an interview or business meeting to hosting an online reading of your book to share with legions of fans worldwide – you do have legions of fans worldwide, right? If not, never fear, social networking will get you there eventually. Starting a "hangout" is just as easy as sending out an invite or enabling a live broadcast with the click of a button. Everyone who is going to participate in your hangout must have a Google account, which virtually everyone does anyway. So are you ready to start hanging out on Google Plus? Start with an informal, public Q & A session for readers or a workshop if your book material lends itself to leading a class or presentation. Hold a private meeting with colleagues – a hangout session might just remind you how much more productive speaking in person can be than bouncing emails back and forth all day long. You could also use a Google Plus Hangout to conduct interviews pertaining to research for your upcoming book. Or, if you're ready to have an all-out celebration, have a virtual book launch party complete with contests and/or prizes to spice things up. This can be especially beneficial if you have a widespread audience and minimal funds to do a worldwide tour to connect with readers.

Ustream (ustream.tv)

Ustream is a website that consists of a network of diverse channels providing a platform for video streaming events online.

For writers, it is especially useful for live video streaming events such as book readings. Whatever show you choose to create, during your broadcast on Ustream, viewers can communicate back to you (and talk to each other) via an optional chat room. They can also leave comments and rate your show.

This feature is a great asset for writers to connect with their reading community because it lets you get instant feedback from your audience and field questions in real time. By recording your show, you can also make it available for viewing later.

Ustream provides production and event services for development, performance metrics, tech support, and connectivity services, as well as promotional services like media and ad sales, custom branded Facebook application, and placement on Ustream's mobile apps.

Because it is available on multiple devices (including computers, phones, streaming players, and televisions), you can easily build an entire campaign around the interactive Ustream experience or use Ustream as an enhancement to your promotional efforts.

Basic use of Ustream (for both producers and viewers) is free; there are also premium memberships available for $3.99 per month.

BlogTalkRadio (blogtalkradio.com)

BlogTalkRadio allows anyone, anywhere, the ability to host a live, internet talk radio show simply by using a telephone and a computer. Thousands of shows are available on the site, which is free to use and doesn't require any type of software download.

BlogTalkRadio's unique technology and seamless integration with leading social networks (such as Facebook and Twitter) empowers citizen broadcasters to create and share their original content, their voices, and their opinions in a public worldwide forum. Many businesses also utilize the platform as a tool to extend their brands and join the conversation on the social web, which authors can just as easily do as well.

Through the live chat feature, listeners connect with a community surrounding a show. Other features include an archive (which saves the show automatically and allows the audio files of the shows to be taken as MP3, RSS subscription, or iTunes), customized alerts by email or phone for upcoming shows, and a customizable profile.

Authors can also join their fans into a group and fans can likewise list their favorite shows. You can also copy and paste Flash player and buttons to any blog or web site to promote your show around the web.

In addition to the free hosting features, BlogTalkRadio offers two Premium Host Packages starting at $39/month, and an optional revenue sharing program for participating hosts.

VIDEO

Like live streaming, video sites also offer a great asset to authors promoting their book. Instead of paying for a commercial to air on television—and competing with a bunch of other 30-second spots that look the same—broadcasting on the internet offers the opportunity to creatively connect with your readers through video.

Although they're not broadcast live, video sites still offer the opportunity to share readings of your book with others and document promotional events to share the experience.

YouTube (youtube.com)

Acting as a distribution platform for original content creators and advertisers of all sizes, YouTube allows billions of people to discover, watch, and share original videos. All you need is a phone or webcam to get started by making a video and establishing your channel. Give it relevant tags and an accurate title and description to help people discover it and you're one step closer to reaching the masses.

Videos can be edited directly in YouTube, and no software downloads are required. You can combine video clips, trim the length of your video, add music, and add transitions between video clips prior to releasing your video to the world.

Once uploaded to YouTube, videos can be searched for by topic or browsed by categories of interest. Videos are viewable on computers and mobile phones, and can also be embedded into any website or blog. Users can "like" videos, maintain a list of favorites, share with friends on other social networks (automatically if you link the accounts), and subscribe to receive automatic updates from their preferred channels. A comment stream is maintained below the video player and the quality of the comments can be rated as well.

Writers who really want to utilize the video medium to its fullest potential have the ability to do so with YouTube's bevy of features. For those authors with a multilingual following, you can have YouTube translate the audio of the video and display it as subtitles. Or really reach out and touch your audience by using the increasingly popular 3D technology (available now on certain phone models) to create multi-dimensional videos.

Vimeo (vimeo.com)

Vimeo is a video sharing community that is available as a free service or on an upgraded "Plus" level for $59.95 a year. While the "community" part of Vimeo is optional, that's what sets the site apart from similar video sharing services. After videos are uploaded, members of the Vimeo community can watch and give feedback on each others' work by leaving comments or clicking the 'Like' button. The cream of the crop is decided by staff and are featured on the site as a "Staff Pick" or added to the HD Channel.

Additionally, there are community forums where members can participate in projects with people from across the globe. And it's all done in the name of circulating videos to an ever widening circle and growing your network. While the site was begun by filmmakers, Vimeo now touts itself as a forum for anyone with a camera "and a little motivation"—except for businesses, it's a noncommercial site. There are indeed video professionals on the site, but there are also a host of people making videos with digital cameras from home.

To ensure a pleasant viewing experience for others, Vimeo offers guidelines for video and audio settings to make the uploading experience optimal for everyone.

WRITER-SPECIFIC PLATFORMS

Online Networking

Here's the thing: You're actually at a huge advantage because you've already written a whole book on your subject. This makes you an expert, and at the very least, makes you able to add value to almost any conversation going on around your area of interest. Even if you wrote a fiction novel, chances are you must be very knowledgeable/interested in the genre (whether it's romance, historical fiction, chick lit, mystery, or any of the many others). Same exact thing if you wrote a non-fiction book—if you live with the subject for 300+ pages, you are certainly an expert in your field and can converse/answer questions/add insight into almost any conversation about that subject.

Also, since you're a writer, you are ideally suited to engage in the discussions/conversations that will eventually convince people that they should pay attention to what you have to say, the end result of which will be them buying your book and telling their friends about it.

Since you are a subject matter expert and are (presumably) willing and able to discuss your favorite subject at any given time, we can logically conclude that all you need is to become aware of discussions/questions that are going on, so that you can jump on in there and join the conversation, as they say.

Here are some things you can do right now to get started:

Set Google Alerts. Did you know that Google has a free service where they will send you an email every single day that contains multiple stories on your area of interest? You can try it out by going to http://google.com/alerts. Here is what it looks like:

To get started, just enter the term in the search box that most closely corresponds with your topic or area of interest. Google will then start sending you handy digests of news stories, blog posts, and just about everything else that appeared on the web that day having to do with your specialty. These daily alerts will give you ample "food for thought" for blog posts, let you know what (or who) is hot in your area of interest at the moment, and give you chances to discover new (possibly well-connected) thought leaders in your area.

Find other bloggers and network with them. Right now, go over to http://blogsearch.google.com, and type in a search term that corresponds to your area of expertise. For example, if you wrote a non-fiction book about organic food, type "organic food" into the search and see what comes up. More than likely, you will find someone else who is talking about that subject, and just by going over to their site and leaving a comment, you are officially engaged in an active discussion that will draw people back to your site (and your work). By searching for other sites and bloggers that have similar interests, you are networking in your chosen field.

If you're wondering where you might find relevant blogs, try Comment Hut, which you can find at http://commenthut.com. You'll need to sign up for a "lite" account, which you can then try out to see if you like the service.

A few notes about comments:

- Be polite. When giving negative comments, do not do so lightly — remember, don't be a troll. If you feel the need to offer constructive criticism or to disagree with or debate what someone is saying, ask yourself first if you are going to make yourself less appealing by doing so. We want people to like you and think you're smart, not just know who you are (as with everything, there are exceptions to this, but they are rare). Remember, the point of all this is marketing, not personal interaction and amusement.

- If you like a blogger's style, consider asking them for a guest post on your blog. Offer them one in return.
- When you like a post by someone you follow, post it to your Facebook page, tweet it on Twitter, etc. Do unto others is true in blogging, as with most things. If you do this, they will likely do the same for you on occasion.

- Always remember to leave a "signature" in your comments, meaning your name and a link back to your website. This will lead people who are also participating in the discussion to go back to your site and check out your work. This is the point of leaving comments in the first place!

Join forums/groups and contribute to discussions.
A forum is an internet discussion group where people can post comments and responses about various subjects. For many books, forums relate to a theme or subject matter, where an appropriate posting can help attract readers. You should consider whether the posting is of real value to the members of the forum.

One way to find forums is through Google searches. Note that most blogs allow comments, so an alternative to suggesting a link might be just posting a comment referencing the book. (But remember, the comment will be seen only by people interested in that particular discussion; a link on the blog page may be seen by a larger audience and may stay on the site longer.)

You can also search for Google groups. For example, a Google search for "books" turns up 30 groups with more than 1,000 members, many of which are quite active. This has the advantage of letting you know how many members a group has and how active it is.
http://groups.google.com/

Yahoo has a large collection of discussion groups that don't usually come up in Google searches for the subject. To find these you have to set up a Yahoo account, then go to the groups section of Yahoo and search for them. The search function is not terrific, but some Yahoo groups are very active and will allow you to reach many potential readers.
http://groups.yahoo.com/

AND...ACTION!

We've given you a ton to think about, and you might be hitting an "overwhelm" point. You might even need a break! Let's just say this: From now on, you'll be writing a 500 (or so) word blog post 1–3 times per week. You'll also be tweeting these posts and putting them on your Facebook page. We'd also like to see you put 15 minutes per day into finding and commenting on other people's blogs, so please add that to your "To Do" list. Right now, though, just in case you'd like to trick out your blog with some awesome Search Engine Optimization, we're going to cover the basics of that.

8

SEARCH ENGINE OPTIMIZATION: KEYWORDS AND CONTENT AND METADATA, OH MY!

We were going to leave this chapter out. Really! You've set up your website and social media, you're going to get yourself out there—what more do we want from you? *Now* we want you to learn even more techie stuff? Isn't what you've already done enough?

Actually, yes. There is no need for you to stress yourself out about search engine optimization (SEO), but believe it or not, some people requested this! So, read on if you're curious, but if you're already overwhelmed, definitely save it for later. Sound good?

Oh, and this probably goes without saying, but if your website doesn't have everything in the checklist in Chapter 4 already taken care of, please go back and work on that some more. Search Engine Optimization on a bad website is the equivalent of putting a giant sail on a tiny, leaky boat. Velocity is only going to accelerate the sinking, if you know what we mean. So wait until you're totally confident in your website to start getting fancy with the keywords.

Search Engine Optimization, in case you haven't heard, is the art and science of ranking in Google for keywords that are relevant to your field. Unless you have a name like "John Smith," you probably won't have much trouble showing up on Page One of Google for your own name with just a website and some social media. But then it becomes a question of "Who is Googling you, and how many books does that mean you'll sell?"

What you really want is for your book to show up for relevant terms in your subject, and that is going to take a little bit of skill. You'll use keywords that you find using some free tools to figure out what the popular words are, put those into key places in your site, blog about them, and when you link back to your site from social media, forums, Question & Answer sites, or other people's blogs, you'll use these words.

SEARCH ENGINE OPTIMIZATION IN A NUTSHELL:

-   "Keywords" are the words that people type in to search engines in order to find things, like "dog food" or "locksmith."

- By looking at keywords, you can determine "demand" for your products and services, then you can provide the "supply" on your site.
- The field of "Search Engine Optimization" or SEO, involves finding the strongest keywords for your target audience, and putting them into relevant places in your site so that the site (the "supply") shows up when people type them in (the "demand").

Simple, right? SEO can be something of a rabbit hole, so we're just going to give you two places to look for keywords and some basic instructions on what to do with them in this chapter. If you totally love the search engine game after that, there are books, forums, and websites galore, and you will certainly find new and exciting ways to show up #1 in the search engines.

There are some useful things you can get from keyword research even if you're not planning on becoming a full-on guru. Let's run some reports so you can just get the keywords—what you do with them after that is totally up to you. Keyword research is very useful, whether you're trying to architect a fancy SEO strategy or just want to know what your audience wants to know, so you can blog about those things and tag your posts accordingly.

KEYWORD RESEARCH: START WITH GOOGLE

The first place you should go to look for keywords is the Google Keyword Tool found in AdWords. You will need a Gmail account for this as well (but you already have one of those from your Analytics, right? RIGHT?!).
- Google has a great free tool at:
  https://adwords.google.com/select/KeywordToolExternal
- Start here to get a feel for the types of things people are typing in, and the related phrases that you might not have considered.
- Add interesting words and phrases to your reference list from Chapter 3. You might want to write blog posts about these eventually!

Market Samurai

If you're still reading and this has piqued your interest, the next step will be to do some competitive analysis using Market Samurai. This is a paid program that you will need to download onto your computer, but there is a free trial that we would recommend you get, just so you can get a feel for what it does and whether you'd like to go further.

Market Samurai was released in the past couple of years, and is very efficient at doing in-depth keyword research in an expedited time period. Click

<u>here</u> for the Market Samurai free trial. Market Samurai will help you identify keywords that for which your site will actually rank. Supply + demand = traffic and results!

Download and install the free trial of Market Samurai on your computer, and then come back and we'll tell you more about the settings. Please do not let all the bells and whistles of the software overwhelm or intimidate you—Market Samurai was developed by SEO people for SEO people, so there are many parts of it that will not be relevant to you. Just focus on the goal of getting great keywords for your site, and don't worry about the rest.

Once you've downloaded Market Samurai and set it up (systems vary, so please consult their help section for specific questions with installation), the first screen you'll see will look like this:

Title your project with the overall "theme" or subject of your book. Examples: "dog training," "stay at home moms" or "websites." Then click "Update," then "Keyword Research."

Other settings: Language = English, Country = United States (unless you intend to serve a more international audience), Adult Content = no (unless you have some).

On the next screen, you'll click the "Generate Keywords" button. This button will produce a list of keywords that are relevant to your first keyword.

Click it now!

Next, you'll eliminate any keywords that are totally irrelevant to your topic, then click the "Keyword Analysis" button to determine the competitiveness of each word (in comparison to other websites on the internet at the time of analysis).

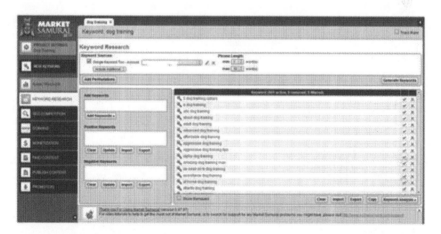

Market Samurai has some pre-sets that are going to eliminate some of the most competitive words. This is a good idea, but if you're truly curious as to the exact numbers for every single word on your list, uncheck all of the boxes, then click the "Analyze Keywords" button.

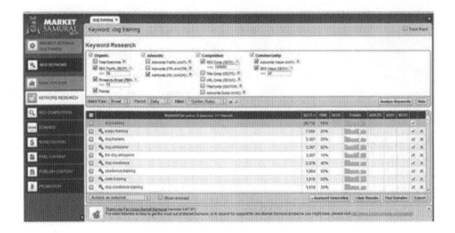

"Searches" refers to how many general searches for this word or phrase occur every month, while "SEOT" is actual search engine traffic, or how many "hits" you could expect to get if you were #1 in Google for that word. "PBR" is "Phrase to Broad," or how closely that term matches the original word or phrase you typed in. Again, don't get overwhelmed! You're just here to find some good keywords and to learn more about the words that will bring your audience to you.

If you see a keyword that has good numbers and totally encompasses your niche, click the "key" symbol next to the word, and it will generate a new list that's based on that one. Be sure to keep a notebook handy, as keyword research will often surprise you with things you had no idea people wanted to know (or to buy).

Repeat this process until you end up with a solid list of keywords that have decent, low-competition numbers but that represent your value proposition to your target audience. Your goal is to develop a list of keywords that you can put into your website.

If you're more of a visual learner, go on over to:
http://www.noblesamurai.com/dojo/marketsamurai/
to watch an amazing series of video tutorials on Market Samurai.

Another great place to find keywords is Wordtracker. Just go to:
www.wordtracker.com and sign up for their free trial. Wordtracker also has an awesome tool called "Keywords to Questions" that is an absolute must if you are a non-fiction writer.
https://freekeywords.wordtracker.com/keyword-questions

Where to Put Those Keywords!

Now that you've done your keyword research (and wasn't it so interesting?), you'll need to go back and put these keywords into your website so that the search engines will associate your site with these words.

These instructions are for people with sites based on WordPress, which gives you the easiest access to your metadata. If your site was built using html, you will need to open up the back-end with a program like Dreamweaver or have your designer/developer do it for you. This is another reason we recommend people switch over to WordPress!

To put your keywords into your site, you'll need a plugin called "Wordpress SEO Pack by Yoast." This plugin is free, and you can find it at: http://wordpress.org/extend/plugins/wordpress-seo/.

Install and activate this SEO plugin, then follow the prompts to set it up. You will be using the keyword list you generated using Market Samurai to write descriptions, title tags, and meta information for your website. Make sure to use complete sentences, and use (but don't overuse) your keywords. In the Keywords section, add the top ten words from your Market Samurai list. If there are more keywords on your list, that's no problem—you'll be using those later on your blog.

If you run out of keywords, feel free to go back to Market Samurai to generate new lists based on similar topics/words. The possibilities are endless!

Another change you'll need to make to your WordPress site is your permalink structure, which will allow the blog posts you title with keyword phrases to be seen more easily by the search engines.

Go to Settings on your dashboard, and then choose Permalinks. You'll need to select the "Custom Structure" button, then fill the box in with the following (very small) piece of code: */%category%/%postname%/*

Feel free to copy and paste. If this is too confusing, choose the second button down, which is "Day and Name." This is almost as good, although you'll lose the benefit of having the category name in each post, which is nice for keyword purposes.

For a screenshot of how this should look, visit: http://bookpromotion.com/permalinks.

Great job! You should pat yourself on the back—most writers don't even have a website, and here you are doing your own Search Engine Optimization!

9
YOUR SOCIAL MEDIA TO-DO LIST

TWITTER

OK, so—your profile is set up, right? You have a link in your profile to your website or blog where someone can actually buy your book, you have a profile photo up there, and you're ready to go.

Just checking. Never waste a potential social media lead! If you don't have this stuff set up yet, please go back to Part One and refer to the Twitter Setup section.

Now that you are on Twitter—what do you actually DO there? There are several things to do there, but remember the basic premise is to engage and converse, not shout "Buy my book!" One of the first things to do is find potential people with similar interests that are relevant to your book. You do this by searching. People who have stated these interests in their bio will come up, as will people who have recently tweeted those terms. Remember, you want to sell your book, which means you need to focus on interacting with people who are likely to buy it. They will then find you interesting, click through to your site, and buy your book! So, find the people and follow them. Some of them will follow you back. Now you are off and running!

Following and following back

You can follow almost anyone you want on Twitter. Most Twitter accounts are open and let anyone follow them. Follow people who look interesting and who you believe will be interested in you. When people follow you first, decide if you want to follow them back. As a general rule, it is polite to follow back, unless you think it is spam, or there is a reason you don't think you want to read their tweets.

Note: You should be following LESS people than you have following you. Nothing gives you away as an amateur faster than having 400 followers, but you're following 2,000 people. (This is Twitter's follow limit for those with under 2,000 followers—they'll let you follow more when you get over 2,000 people following you). Keep an eye on who follows you, and unfollow those that don't (We use www.manageflitter.com for this).

Hashtags

Hashtags are a way unique to Twitter of identifying things within the broader Twitter-sphere (no, we did not just make that term up). They look like this: #hashtag and sometimes like this: #thingsthatarehashtags. People use hashtags to find other people who are discussing a topic. Unfortunately, there is no dictionary or encyclopedia of Hashtags. You have to figure them out by watching your Twitter stream, and through trial and error. A sample tweet using a hashtag might look like this:

 Matthew Inman @Oatmeal   2 hrs
Thanks to everyone at #SXSW who came to my keynote. I was really stressed out and nervous beforehand.
Followed by Network Marketing and 1 other
Expand

@ Symbols

Notice in the above tweet that the writer's Twitter handle (next to the @) is used at the end of the tweet. That is how he will know that he was being tweeted about! That will also allow him to retweet the tweet if he would like. This helps him get things in his Twitter stream, while also showing the world that hey, someone was talking about me! This is also how you have a public conversation with someone or several people. Simply add their @name to your tweet, and they will see it.

Note: Using the @symbols of famous people is not that likely to get you a response unless what you send is REALLY interesting. Mostly, it is going to be a waste of time. On the other hand, using the hashtag of a famous person will connect you with those people who are fans and interested in them—an important distinction if you think your topic is of interest to a particular fan base.

Retweeting

Retweeting is polite, good Twitter etiquette, and gives you a way of putting more tweets out with very little effort. Simply put, if you see something interesting, or that you want to promote, click the retweet button. People like to be retweeted, so if you can, do it often and it will help broaden your follower base and gain more interest.

And now for the Twitter checklist. Please put this on your list of things to do for 15 minutes every morning and evening.

1. Log in to Twitter.
2. Go to http://search.twitter.com.
3. Click "Advanced Search Options".
4. Specify the search terms, like local farms, or organic milk, and limit the search to your local area. You can also search by conversational topic, or hashtag, by simply typing in #localmilk or #organic or anything like that (keep it to the local area, though).
5. This search will turn up a list of people who are talking about that subject right that minute. Perhaps you would like to follow a few of those people, especially if they look like they would be interested in your book.
6. Begin @replying to each and every one of them with actual insight on what they're saying. In order to do this, you will need to click the individual name of each person who is Tweeting, and then click Reply on that particular tweet.

Here is an excellent article on Twitter How-to from Mashable:
http://mashable.com/guidebook/twitter/

If Twitter is really your thing, you might want to also check these sites, which are gaining popularity as Twitter directories (see the Bonus section for a full analysis of each of these services and what they offer). The great thing about sites like these is that they break Twitter users into groups, such as by interest, geographic area, or by number of followers. If you wrote a book that's set in Delaware, for example, you might want to follow people who live in Delaware.

http://twellow.com
http://wefollow.com
http://tweetbeep.com

FACEBOOK

Now that you have set up your author page (go back to part one and set that up if you haven't) what the heck do you do with it? The simple answer: put stuff out there. You are trying to set up a dialog with your readers, fans and potential readers. This is your ability to be human and accessible. So how does that work exactly?

Priority number one, post stuff! What do you post? Things like this:

- Blog posts (further evidence that you need a blog)
- Events
- Photos of you at events
- Photos of your book in various interesting places

Here is some more information about photo tagging on Facebook: http://www.facebook.com/notes/facebook-pages/feature-launch-photo-tagging-for-pages/10150168953654822.

More information about general Status Tagging: http://mashable.com/2009/09/14/how-to-facebook-status-tagging/.

If you are posting interesting things and you have people reading the posts, you will start seeing comments. Respond to them! Check in and respond to comments when you can. Your readers will appreciate this.

Using Facebook "as" your Fan Page, you are able to comment on other Fan Pages and profiles. We would recommend using Facebook as your page (not yourself) as often as possible. In case you don't know how to switch from using Facebook as your profile to using it as a page, you'll just need to go to the Account tab at the far right, then click on Use Facebook as (Page Name).

Chances are you're already familiar with Facebook because you use it to connect with friends and family. If so, that's great! Your Facebook Fan Page will be a logical extension of that, and you'll already be familiar with the user interface, so it will be much easier for you. Also, if you're wondering, it IS ok to mention your book/website on your Facebook page—Facebook knows you have a life, and of course sometimes you're going to cross the line between business and personal. You do need a Fan Page, though, because while Facebook will allow you to mention business-related things on an occasional basis, the Fan Page is where this is actually allowed, and you'll be able to keep in contact directly with your fans this way, instead of having to add them all as personal friends.

PINTEREST

As we mentioned during the section on setup, Pinterest has taken off very quickly. From a functional perspective, this means that there will be a lot of big changes in a very short period of time while the folks at Pinterest try to figure out exactly how to monetize and expand their product. We are aiming to update this book a couple of times a year, but that may not be quite quickly enough to keep up with the flow. In the interim, we will post articles on bookpromotion.com to keep you up to speed.

How do you know whether this is a useful social media platform for your work? Well, in truth, because it is still evolving, it is hard to say where the sweet spot is from a demographic perspective. It certainly took off with the fans of scrapbooking first, so women are more prevalent than men. It is also clear that fashion, food, travel, and inspirational quotes top the most popular topics.

Pinterest is set up as though you have a series of bulletin boards. They have helped get you started by creating some of the typical ones that folks create. They are organized by topic, such as "Food". You can (and should) create your own boards grouped by your own topics. For example, a board titled "Books On My Nightstand" or "Other Authors". From that point on, you will pin things to those boards, just as though you had taken the photo/article/item and pinned it up with a thumbtack. Because your goal is to attract and interact with people who will read and like your book, you should think about what types of things you will want to track as you go, and set up boards appropriately. If you write about travel, you might want boards for your favorite countries. If you write Chick-Lit, you will want things like Recipes and Funny Stuff. It is hard to go wrong, so even just starting simply and pinning things that interest you personally will get you going. Honestly, it is exactly that simple.

Just as with Twitter, on Pinterest you "follow" friends or people that you find interesting. Just like Twitter (where you re-tweet), you can "re-pin" things that people you are following have pinned or pin your own material. Head on over, and start poking around, and follow some people. Pinterest helps you out by making some recommendations - no reason not to take them! The simplest way to start is by re-pinning things that look interesting. Pretty picture of France, sure why not, pin that up in "Places I Want to See". Recipe for roasted cauliflower, yes please, pin that on to "Food I Should Eat" (whereas the recipe for chocolate cake might go on "Food I Know I Shouldn't Eat"). Many of the pins you are seeing are not static images. If you click on the graphic, you will be taken to the website/recipe/article behind the pin.

You can also "Like" pins that interest you, or comment on them. Just as with the other platforms we describe here, since your goal is to interact on topics that are going to overlap with your readership, you should try to do more than just repin and throw up new pins, get in there and get talking to other pinners!

If you have followed our instructions, you have installed the Pin-It button to your browser, and you should see the Pinterest "P" logo on the toolbar at the top. This is what makes Pinterest truly interesting to those of us using it for business. As you are reading an article, say a blog post you wrote, you can simply click this symbol to pin the article in question straight in to Pinterest. Be sure to describe what you are pinning in a way to help people understand why they would want to do the same thing. (Hint, this is another good reason to use photos and illustrations in your blog posts, as this gives a good visual for Pinterest.) Once something is pinned in this way, the photo becomes a clickable link to the content. You can also add the url or a shortened link within the description of the content.

Now – this may go without saying, do not merely pin and repin your own book cover, reviews, etc. The point of all of the social media sites is interaction and content. Pinterest is no different.

LINKEDIN

LinkedIn is not going to be necessary for most fiction authors, at least on a day-to-day basis. However, you do want to at least have a profile with the basic info out there. You are a professional author —remember to list that as one of your jobs! You want to be taken seriously, and one of the things other people use when deciding whether to take you seriously or not is LinkedIn. Non-fiction writers or writers deeply tied to a cause, get on and start participating! If you have a business book, we hope LinkedIn isn't news to you, because every serious businessperson we know is already on and using LinkedIn. If you are not, it is by no means too late. Get your profile completed and get moving!

The easiest ways to participate are as follows:
- Groups—people who have a similar interest or background (i.e. if the book is on entrepreneurial endeavors, search for these groups and join).
- Q&A and discussions—best if you stick to answering relevant questions versus chiming in on everything. You want to be seen as an expert.
- Business pages—if you have a related business (i.e. consulting), set up a business page on LinkedIn.

For a long and truly ridiculous list of all the social media properties in the entire world, please visit Knowem, at http://knowem.com. If you are so inclined (or you have a teenager on summer break who owes you some work hours), feel free to register your own name on as many of these properties as you'd like. And remember: *Always* link them back to your main website. Later, you will link them all together to form a media empire.

That's it (for now!). As long as you have a website and are interacting with people on social media on a daily basis, you will be building your audience in anticipation of your book launch (or sending people back to your website to buy your book). Here is a handy checklist that will help you build blogging and social media into your day so it becomes habitual, like flossing or working out.

YOUR BLOG: ACTION LIST

1–3 times per week:
- Write a post for your blog, and/or guest blog posts for others. (If you prefer, this can also be audio or video if you're technically oriented in that way.)
- Make sure this blog post also gets sent out through your social media, like Twitter/Facebook/LinkedIn.
- Read/comment on other people's blogs with a link that goes back to your website.

SOCIAL MEDIA: DAILY ACTION LIST

Try to dedicate at least 15 minutes per day to your social media efforts. You will be learning the ropes, and it is very important that you keep at it so you get used to how it all works.

If you have 15 minutes:
- Log in to Twitter.
- Check mentions, @replies, saved searches, keywords. Follow new people back. Retweet noteworthy blog posts/quotes from friends.
- Reach out to 2–3 people with similar interests.
- Log in to Google Plus.
- + 1 some people's posts, post up (or at least share) some interesting content. Interact!!

If you have 15 more minutes:
- Log in to Facebook. Check messages, comment on 1–3 friends' pages (or comment back on other's comments to your previous postings). Post new content such as photos or links to interesting things.

Got more time? Great! Here are a few more things you can do.
- Write more blog posts.
- Log in to the book sites, add books to your bookshelves, and/or interact with other users there.
- Answer questions on Yahoo Answers, in Linked In groups, and in any forums where you're a member. Every little bit counts, and be sure to always point back to your own website, where people will find your blog, like your writing, and want to buy your books.

10
What to Do on the Book Sites

In many ways, the book sites (Amazon, Goodreads, Shelfari, and LibraryThing) overlap with the Social Networking platforms like Twitter and Facebook. But since they are book specific, they are often a quite comfortable place for authors to start. We want to make sure that in addition to checking on and updating your social media profiles on a regular basis, you're stopping by the major book sites, keeping your profiles updated and interacting with potential readers and fellow book-lovers. Who wouldn't want to do that?

Amazon.com

Yes, we're back to Amazon again, and why not? It's like a Swiss Army knife—store, suite of tools, and leader in cutting-edge sales techniques, all rolled into one. You will spend a lot of time on this site. Some things you can control, whereas others you must merely accept. Here are some of the things you're going to be looking at anyway, so we'll go ahead and comment on them so you're prepared.

Reviews

Some of this you probably already know, but we don't want to miss a step, so bear with us if this is rudimentary to you. Statistically, books with no reviews sell far less (and are usually poorly ranked), so you do want to get some reviews out there. Here are the things to remember when it comes to book reviews:

- **Do not** review your own book
- **Do not** pay for reviews
- **Do not** respond to negative reviews
  *Note that the only exception to this is if there is a functional question or comment you can address. I.e. someone complains about formatting and you have released a new version with the formatting repaired.

You do need to drum up *some* reviews, so what should you do, you might ask? While you're waiting for media outlets to release their reviews (this mostly applies to you if your book is with a traditional publisher), get some people who have read your book to leave a review.

- **Do** ask anyone who has read your book to please do you a favor and review it. In the last version of this book, we indicated that "friends and family are fine" as a starting point for reviews. Now, technically, that is still true – but with a caveat: Amazon has begun to proactively remove reviews provided by close friends or family members of authors. They will also remove reviews from anyone who has a "financial interest" in the book, and we can tell you from direct experience that this means authors who hail from the same publishing house. So, whomever you ask for reviews, they must be well written, not too familiar (i.e. avoid using an authors first name) and not clearly from one of these sources. Aside from that, interpret the policy as you will and hope for the best. **Do** send requests for reviews to anyone you can think of who would enjoy your book. This includes people you know, friends of friends, and even people you don't know that may have reviewed similar books. This is where having a few copies of your book sitting on your desk will come in handy.
- **Do** post reminders about your book on your social media, call in favors to any media people that you might know, and look back on the list of people and interests you made in Chapter 3 to remind yourself about potential reviewers.

Note that most reviewers who receive a free copy will indicate this fact—this is considered proper form. There are also guidelines for reviewers on Amazon, so check them out and DO NOT violate them! In case you would like to read them, here's a link:
http://www.amazon.com/gp/community-help/customer-reviews-guidelines

We have even seen some authors include postcards in books they're selling at events, pointing people back to the book sites and encouraging those who enjoyed the book to leave a review.

One more thing you should know about is the Amazon Reviewers. Getting reviews from some of Amazon's top reviewers can seriously boost credibility of your book. Top Reviewers have a special badge next to their usernames, such as Top 1,000 Reviewer, Top 500 Reviewer, Top 50 Reviewer, Top 10 Reviewer, or #1 Reviewer.

Rankings of the Top Reviewers are determined by a point system based on the number of reviews written and the number of positive votes those reviews receive (when people click "Yes" in response to, "Was this review helpful to you?"). Top Reviewers are regular Amazon customers who simply enjoy reading and critiquing lots of books. Many of them review several books per week—sometimes at the invitation of an author or publisher, but usually based on their personal interests. Amazon Top Reviewers compete furiously to climb the rankings ladder (probably because being at the top means you get barraged with free books and requests for reviews!).

Here's the catch: Most of them are so backlogged in their reading, if they decide to read your book, it will be weeks or months before they post a review. And most of them receive so many requests, they can't even respond to them all. So while this may be a good tool, it can also be a waste of time. Put this towards the bottom of your marketing to-do list, especially if you are not starting well ahead of your book launch, and/or will not have advance copies for reviewers.

If you do want to pursue this route, how do you find these super reviewers? Start with books that are similar in genre or topics to yours, read their reviews, and find reviewers you would like to investigate further. Clicking on a reviewer's username takes you to his or her Amazon profile, which contains biographical and other information that has been posted. Some reviewer profiles will explain what types of books they prefer, if the reviewer accepts unsolicited books, and some even provide a website or e-mail address. Carefully screen out reviewers whose profile indicates they aren't interested in your book's topic.

You can find the list of Top Reviewers here:
http://www.amazon.com/reviews/top-reviewers/ref=cm_pdp_top_reviewers

Your Amazon Ranking

This ranks second for most authors (after reviews) in the "obsessive monitoring" category. The theory is that you can track interest in the book through Amazon ratings by looking at its ranking number. This number is literally the rank of your book when compared to the other 5 million books on Amazon, so lower is better (i.e. you would like your book to be #1, not #5,000,000). These ratings **help** show if a book is selling, but they do not exactly reflect sales rank. Amazon won't explain precisely how the ratings are generated but it has to do with sales and also with the frequency with which the web page is viewed. It probably also has something to do with other mysterious algorithmic voodoo involving purchase patterns or inclusion in guides and lists. This is good news for you, because as you go through your social networking to-do list and get more people to go back to your site, more people will click through to your book (and hopefully buy it), which should help boost it in the rankings.

We know you're going to look at this stuff (all authors do it), but here is the reality of the situation (and why should stop checking Amazon so much): There is virtually nothing you can do to change this number, aside from doing your best to get yourself out there and sell as many books as possible. The second reality is this: It is not totally clear that having a better ranking makes any difference until you make it all the way to the top 100. Once you hit that level, you get special attention and promotion automatically by Amazon. So really, our best advice is to just market your book the best you possibly can, and try not to focus too much on this number!

Tags & Likes

Interestingly, between versions one and two of this book, both Tags and Likes were removed as features on Amazon. On the one hand, good news for you, as there is less you need to worry about doing. On the other, bad news, because it is one less thing you can use to bring attention to your book.

Guides (was Listmania)

In fact, in some areas of Amazon, Listmania appears to still exist. Our impression is that it is being phased out in favor of Guides, but it is rather hard to say. In general, the newer feature is the one they intend to focus on, regardless, and therefore so should you.

Not surprisingly, this too has changed since this book first came out. It appears that Listmania has been morphed into the new feature called Guides. Like Listmania, anyone can create one, and they can include just about anything on Amazon. They are limited to 50 products, but include far more detail and educational opportunity on the topic at hand than the simple "lists" did. You can see the creation tool (and a sample guide) here:
http://www.amazon.com/gp/richpub/syltguides/create/

As before, you have two choices: create your own, or try to get included in one that already exists. If you create your own, be sure it is relevant to your topic. If you ask for inclusion, not only should the guide be relevant, it should also be active. Be sure you check the views, and look for the most recent modification to determine whether the list is still active.

While it does make sense to stay aware of what's going on with your status on Amazon, don't let it become a distraction! Check in there occasionally to make sure that everything is ok, put a few feelers out for reviews or inclusion in lists, and take a peek at your sales rank, then BACK AWAY. You have that whole to-do list to get through, after all—you don't have time to obsess.

KDP Select & Pricing Promotions

We advise authors, especially those who are going the indie route, to enroll their books in the KDP Select program. This means that authors of a traditional publishing house will have no control over whether they are enrolled or not. The same is true of pricing, as only those who load the book into the systems can control the price of their books.

GOODREADS

Goodreads is currently the leader in the book social media space. You've already (ideally) created your account, and when you log in, you'll keep your online library up to date, organize it by shelves, and add reviews. You can also add friends, join or form groups and otherwise interact with other bookish people.

Goodreads is fun, the people there like to talk about books, and it deserves a little attention. Do we think you will sell thousands of books using Goodreads? Honestly, probably not. Do we think you could <u>prevent</u> yourself from selling thousands by ignoring Goodreads completely? Yes. Absolutely. It should definitely be part of your marketing toolkit/portfolio.

Here are some other things you can do on Goodreads (besides talking about books, of course):

- **Giveaways.** Within Goodreads, you may sign up to give away a certain number of copies of your book over a certain period of time. This is a good way to get your book some visibility, as most people who sign up for the giveaway will put your book on their to-read shelf, and people who receive books usually leave a review (if they don't, they can't participate in further giveaways). But (and you can file this under "good to know" if nothing else) many people sign up for all the giveaways, regardless of the book's genre or description, so you're going to end up with a few reviews that start out "if I liked this genre of book…." We agree—we're not sure why someone would sign up to receive a book in a genre they don't enjoy, but let's hope they know enough to give you a decent review once they've read it!

- **Book recommendations**. On Goodreads, you can recommend books to your friends, which you should try to do only sporadically with your own book. Here's why: If they truly are your friends (not random people that you don't know who have friended you or vice versa, which is quite common on Goodreads) then they already know about your book. If they are essentially strangers, they are more likely to be annoyed at the suggestion until you have actually established a rapport of some sort with them. Remember, you are not supposed to be randomly shouting "Buy my book!" in any of these contexts. Rather, you're building a relationship and platform where that will happen naturally.

- **Groups**. There are many groups on Goodreads, and most are loosely organized around topics, genres, or authors. If your book is relevant to the discussion, and their individual policies allow it, you may post your book as a Suggested Read. Be careful to respect the various groups requests with respect to promotion or you may be in trouble!

- **Lists**. There are many, many lists on Goodreads, and you can add your book to lists as appropriate (again, don't overdo!). It's much better to cultivate a fan base or group of online friends who will do it for you!

For truly well-known work and authors, many folks are entertained by creating and taking quizzes. We would not suggest doing this until your work is well known, however, and by the time that happens, someone else will do it for you! Cultivate your fan base, and eventually someone will make a quiz out of one of your books, which will amuse you to no end.

LIBRARYTHING AND SHELFARI

We have debated about how deeply to dive into each of these technologies. To be honest, they are secondary in market share to Goodreads and each has unique features, and we don't want you to get too bogged down with any one thing, get frustrated, and quit. Don't do that! When in doubt, go back to our old mantra: Blog. Post. Tweet. Repeat!

That said, Library Thing and Shelfari both have a devoted following, and are worth checking out to see if their character and overall "vibe" are compatible with yours. Anything you enjoy using is bound to be more successful for you! With each of these, just get in there, set up your profile, look around, and talk to people about books (yours and others you like). You will quickly be able to get a feel for whether one (or both) are worth your time. If they are, add them to your to-do list!

A note about LibraryThing giveaways: Unlike Goodreads, there are two giveaway programs on LibraryThing. The first is the Early Readers program. This program is only available when a publisher communicates with LibraryThing, and they only take pre-publication books without a special arrangement. Self-published books can only be offered via their other giveaway program, Member Giveaways. Both programs tend to result in reviews, but obviously the Early Reader program is more popular as people feel they are being given a special sneak peek into your book before anyone else.

If you are with a large publisher who does ARCs (advance reader copies) they may already have a program in place to work with LibraryThing, so be sure to check before doing a Member Giveaway. If you are with a smaller publisher, Early Readers may be challenging to get into without some special arrangements, and there is no need for you to waste time pursuing that. Don't stress about it. While we do want you to have knowledge of (and a presence on) the book sites, it's not the end of the world if you don't get in to Early Readers. In fact, the more you diversify in your social media and other PR activities, the less that missing out on any one of those methods will seem like the end of the world. Keep plugging away, connecting with readers, writing blog posts, and spreading the word about your book. You'll get there!

11
TALK IT OUT!

Still don't have enough to do? We've got even MORE places where you can share your writing and expertise while getting people back to your site. We could keep going on this stuff all day!

Get Out Your Chapter 3 List (again)

Remember back in Chapter 3, when we had you make a list of all the websites, forums, networks, and groups where people who are interested in your topic congregate? Now is the time to break out that list and make sure that you have a presence on each and every one of them, especially where you can participate in discussions that demonstrate just how well-informed and intelligent you are. Go get that list now and put some work into it. Make notes about more groups/contacts you find there. Repeat.

REDDIT (REDDIT.COM)

Reddit originally had the reputation for being the "bad boy" of the social networking scene, and was known more for controversial content. That has changed quite a bit. Although you can still find the controversy if you like it, it is also a great place to discover breaking news, and all manner of things—like your book!

Reddit users provide all of the content and decide through voting what's good and what's junk. Links that receive community approval bubble up to the top, so the front page is constantly in motion and (hopefully) filled with fresh, interesting links. There is also a cap on how many things users can post per time increment to prevent spamming. By default, new users are subscribed to a selection of the most popular categories, but the experience can be personalized by subscribing to ones that appeal to you. After doing so, the front page will change to show a customized listing tailored to your interests.

Reddit is made up of hundreds of sub-communities, each focused on a specific topic, which can distinguish themselves through their policies.

These sub-communities also feature moderators that help configure parameters for their community, remove objectionable links and comments, and ban spammers or other abusive users. The niche community aspect and cap on posts helps filter out spammers just trying to push their website to the top themselves (instead of allowing the community to decide what's really good), which may lead some authors to find this service to be a preferred choice.

So how do you know if Reddit is right for you? Well, like just about everything in this book, one size does not fit all. You have to examine your options, and decide what looks, feels and fits best for you. Obviously, we have ideas on which things are most successful, and those things are highlighted. Reddit may become your preferred network, or maybe not. Check it out and decide for yourself!

WattPad

WattPad is a platform for posting your writing via computer, tablet or phone. It's a free outlet into a worldwide audience where you can be anonymous or fly with the freedom of a pen name as you venture into that non-fiction garden writing career about which you always secretly dreamed. Or something a little racier, whatever is your scene. But WattPad isn't only for writers hoping to put some work out into the world under a pseudonym. Because of its social aspect, WattPad can be a good place to get some feedback on that new novel or test out your non-fiction piece in the real world. It's also a place to collaborate, and perhaps co-write, with other authors. You might also find yourself plucked from the crowd by a publisher who stumbles upon your work while perusing the site. But you don't have to sit around waiting for someone else. WattPad can be used as a promotional tool for that self-published book of yours right now. With a membership tally in the millions, WattPad offers an audience ready to not only read your book, but to participate in the storytelling process and give you input on everything from plot twists to cover design which will ultimately help make your next book a success from the start with your built-in audience chomping at the bit for your next piece. For a great piece about a writer who broke out using WattPad, refer to: http://bookpromotion.com/how-i-did-it-by-brittany-geragotelis/

PATH

Path is dubbed as a personal journal in the form of an app for your iPhone or Android. Basically it is a multimedia timeline (or "path") similar to a Facebook timeline that consists of various updates and interactions between your friends and family. Also similar to Facebook, you can choose to follow the personal paths of others. The major difference between Path and Facebook, however, is that Path is currently a mobile-only app and was designed with personal, private sharing in mind. A personal intent which is particularly obvious with the 150-friend limit. On a personal level a lot of people may be flocking to Path this year as the kind of anti-Facebook – a return to meaningful, intimate interaction with people you actually know in real life as friends. But even on a personal level, you're still a writer, so Path might be the place for you to share some things about the book writing or promoting experience that you don't want to share with the masses. Surrounded by true friends and family (instead of fans) it also might be a good place for you to request some help or give inside scoops. The place functionality is a good way for your close friends and family to keep tabs on you during your world tour – or while you're headed to that indie book store down the block. And, if you really want to go into detail with your best buds, there is even a feature to let folks know when you're going to sleep or what time you're waking up. Finally, an app to let your mom know how late you've been out drinking away your writers' block sorrows.

QUESTION/ANSWER SITES

Question/Answer sites offer an opportunity to establish yourself as an expert in your field. Or, if being an expert on a certain topic isn't directly related to your book (or of any interest to you, for that matter), you can still utilize the medium by answering questions with a bit of humor, or based on situations or characters in your book. And of course, it's yet another opportunity to get your name out there and link back to your site.

On the flip side, browsing through some of the questions that go through people's minds might be the spark you need to get you started on your next book.

Askville.com

A subsidiary of Amazon.com, Askville is a free question and answer site. Users ask a question and receive answers from the community. They can also browse questions in a variety of topics of interest and show appreciation for good answers by giving "thanks." Users are awarded Askville Achievements by asking good questions or receiving several compliments from other users.

You can discover questions that you can help with by following the categories you are interested in or categories that somehow relate to the topic of your book. To answer, you simply type your answer into the box or you can add an attachment or link that's related—something related to your book, perhaps.

Answers.com & WikiAnswers (wikianswers.com)

Answers.com combines community-driven questions and answers with respected and trusted editorial reference books. To answer questions asked by its users, the site either pulls from the collection of community answers or from its reference databases.

There are a couple of ways that authors may choose to get involved in the community by providing answers in their areas of expertise. In the WikiAnswers feature, anyone can ask, answer, edit, or collaborate on answers in thousands of categories of questions of a more unique or social nature. ReferenceAnswers, on the other hand, is the place for trusted editorial sources to answer simple questions of "who" or "what" with reference information pulled from hundreds of trusted licensed sources. There are also sections for Video Answers and International Answers.

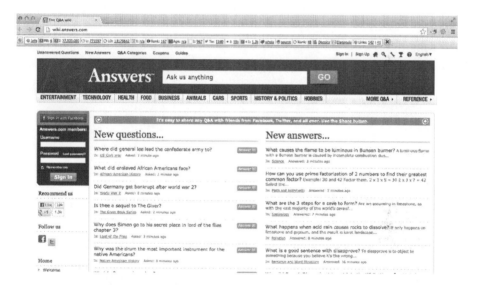

wikiHow (wikihow.com)

Another site is wikiHow, a collaborative effort to build and share the world's largest, highest quality how-to manual. Similar to eHow, its focus is on learning how to do something. But because it's a wiki, anyone can write or edit a page on the site, so what you originally write may not wind up being the final product. Each edit can be seen on the list of recent changes, which is reviewed constantly by volunteer editors.

Yahoo! Answers (answers.yahoo.com)

Yahoo! Answers is a place where people ask and answer questions on any topic. Check out the category list on the left side of the page to find open questions regarding a topic you know something about or perhaps have written about to begin participating in the community. Extra points are earned by having your answer chosen as the best.

Unlike other question/answer sites that are trying to position themselves as a very specific type of reference tool, Yahoo! Answers is a little more informal, so this could be a good place to have some fun with your answers and get users excited about your book through your amazing sense of humor.

This site aggregates all the answer sites, for your convenience: http://www.refseek.com/directory/answers.html

So go, start a profile, and answer people's questions as the expert that you are. When you're setting up your account, be sure to use the same name, biographical info, photo, and link back to your website that you've been consistently using across all of your other online properties.

ARTICLE SITES

Authors can use article sites to establish their expertise in an area and promote their own website. It's a simple but powerful way to share your interests, build your online identity and credibility, and connect with new readers and friends. As a side note, it is actually not kosher to put "duplicate content" (i.e. the same article) on a bunch of different article sites. The best idea would be to look around a few of these sites, decide which one you like the best, and focus on that one. This way you can go back to that site over and over again and build up your credibility and expert status by writing articles. If you've done freelance work for article sites before (such as Demand Media or Suite101), you probably understand the format, but you're not getting paid directly for writing these (at least not much)— rather, the purpose of these articles will be to get you credibility and new readers.

If writing articles is something that interests you, definitely get this e-book by Connie Ragen Green, who is an expert on the EzineArticles.com platform (as well as several other things).

Ezine Articles (ezinearticles.com)

EzineArticles.com is a matching service that brings real-world experts and ezine publishers together. Email newsletter publishers looking for fresh content use the site to find articles for inclusion in their next newsletter. Expert authors and writers are able to post their articles to be featured within the site, which includes a searchable database of hundreds of thousands of original articles.

Each article is reviewed by a human editor (*not* by some type of software) usually within 2–10 business days. Articles are managed by Ezine's proprietary management software designed to give maximum exposure to the online audience and email newsletter publishers, while the author maintains exclusive rights to the content.

EzineArticles encourages authors to use their site to promote themselves and receive a massive increase in exposure, a boost in credibility, and a way to direct visitors back to your website.

Anyone who publishes your article in their email newsletter is required to include your mini-biography or website contact information and is not allowed to alter or edit your article in any way without obtaining your permission first.

For writers who meet quality standards consistently, Ezine extends "platinum unlimited status," which allows the writer to send in unlimited articles and receive priority article review processing speed.

Article sites offer a unique opportunity for authors to build their portfolio, hone their skills, get in touch with their audience, and take advantage of free advertising all in one. And authors might even get paid for it on some sites.

By taking a little time to write an article in your area of expertise or perhaps on the subject matter of your fictional story, you can find an easy way to promote your own website and personal brand. Most article sites will also syndicate your work as long as it credits back to you, and that can increase your readership and help you connect with new people.

Article marketing can be a great way to boost your credibility, which is especially helpful for authors who are seeking to establish themselves as an expert on a particular topic.

Article Alley (articlealley.com)

Article Alley offers a free article directory as a way to help authors promote and syndicate their content—in article form. It's free for writers to sign up, and attracts everyone from novice writers to business professionals writing about their area of expertise. This serves to draw people back to their own websites (which could be the case for authors as well). Overall it is an easy way to publish your work and attract readers in a large community. As one of the main free content websites on the internet, Article Alley provides an opportunity for authors and promoters to potentially have their work read by millions.

Work published on Article Alley is free to be republished by webmasters worldwide, provided that all original links remain within the article and all credit remains with the original article author—this can potentially help increase traffic to your site as well.

It's not really a strict publishing process. Basically as long as a submitted article complies with the guidelines, it will be published.

Articles Base (articlesbase.com)

ArticlesBase is a free site where you can publish your articles or others can mine content for their website, ezine, or newsletter.

Like most article sites, ArticlesBase works as free advertising for whoever is writing the article. The author bio box is a tool to promote your own website and personal brand that can be used to gain unlimited visitors to your website. The syndication possibilities can drastically increase your readership, especially by harnessing the power of RSS feeds. This can sometimes help you to connect with people you may not have been able to previously reach with your work.

It also works as a way to boost your credibility, which could be especially helpful for authors who are seeking to establish themselves as an expert in a specific subject.

What makes ArticlesBase particularly appealing to authors is the extensive statistics, which allow you to better target your audience. Also important to note is that articles that have been submitted to ArticlesBase aren't removed, which means that your articles can continue to bring traffic to your site for years to come and could get picked up and reprinted years later.

Yahoo! Voices (voices.yahoo.com)

Yahoo! Voices (previously Associated Content) is another way to share your knowledge and passion with a multitude of people via written content, photographs, or videos. With this unique medium you can either publish based on your own desired topics, or claim opportunities from the Assignment Desk in areas like Yahoo! News, Yahoo! Sports, Yahoo! Finance, omg!, Shine, and Associated Content. Overall, the Yahoo! network reaches more than 600 million unique visitors each month.

eHow.com (ehow.com)

Another popular site is eHow, with more than 30 categories of content aimed at creating a free, one-stop online resource for "life's challenges," with articles written on a variety of topics.

With popular subjects such as cooking, decorating, fixing, planning, gardening, budgeting, or fashion, eHow could be a cool way for authors with books related to any of those topics to establish themselves as a true expert in the field. And you can think outside the box. Maybe you studied gardening to get some details straight on your fiction book—even that could provide an opportunity for you to write an article related to the subject.

Do keep in mind that the whole point of eHow is the "how." If you can write an article that relates to how someone can get something done, go for it!

Gather (gather.com)

Gather is a website where members can talk about their own views and join in conversations with others who share their interests. Gather works with hundreds of freelance writers who start thousands of conversations on the site each month. Become one of those writers to start a conversation on something related to your book or your work.

Scribd (scribd.com)

Scribd is trying to position itself as the largest book club on the planet. Anyone can join in on conversations taking place on any topic imaginable— everything from vampire fan fiction to crossword puzzles. If you get on there and spark up the conversation, your book could be the next hot topic.

Millions of people contribute to the conversations happening on Scribd by commenting, rating, and "Readcasting" to friends on Scribd, Facebook, and Twitter. And in addition to that part of the service, there are two other unique features which make it a full-fledged virtual book club.

For starters, Scribd also developed Float, a unique digital reading service that includes a suite of web and mobile applications that make all your favorite documents, news, blogs, and friend recommendations available anytime and anywhere. Float is personalized to your interests, integrated with social sharing features, and offers a "floating" reading experience across devices.

Scribd also has patent-pending conversion technology which allows anyone to instantly upload and transform any file—including PDF, Word and PowerPoint—into a web document that's discoverable through search engines, shared on social networks, and read on millions of mobile devices. With that, you can upload, organize, and distribute your work on the web and mobile devices, making it a sort of central hub for your written content.

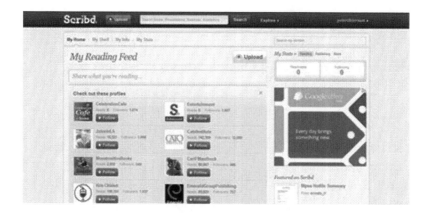

Squidoo (squidoo.com)

Squidoo is a free publishing platform that lets users create "lenses" online. Squidoo's lenses are basically pages, like flyers or signposts or overview articles, which gather everything someone knows about a topic of interest and "snaps it all into focus." The idea is that everyone is an expert on something—be it their hobby, career, or just themselves.

Authors can utilize the site to create a lens about themselves, their blog, or the topic of their book. At the same time they will be offering the reading world at large another opportunity to connect with them.

Many lensmasters earmark their earnings for charity, which could be interesting to combine with your promotional efforts. If you've written a book that centers on the topic of domestic abuse, you could choose to have your revenue stream from Squidoo donated to a non-profit organization that works for that cause and spread the good word on all of your other online mediums.

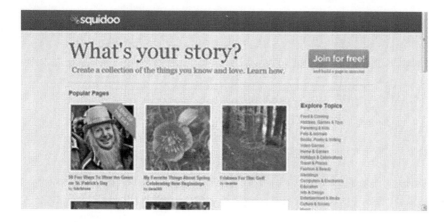

12

PR and Publicity: Old and New

We said we'd get to this eventually, right? The truth is, you really need to get the rest of your network together before you even think about doing things like sending out a press release or pitching yourself to a producer for a possible radio or TV appearance (or even hiring a PR agency to do this for you).

Why?

It all comes back to selling those books. Say you put real effort into sending out a great press release, get yourself an appearance on your local morning radio show as an expert, and in exchange, they give you a mention at the end of the segment. These days, people who listen to the radio are more likely to Google you, go to your website, and (hopefully) buy your book right then when they're thinking about you, rather than writing down (or trying to remember) your name, then looking for you in the bookstore.

See where are we going with this?

The real truth is, the "old" book publicity model (early reviews by big media outlets, book tour, media appearances/mentions) is not nearly as effective as you might think, and that is part of the reason why publishing is right in the middle of a revolution. Yes, it would be great if you could get on the *TODAY* show, but your book can still be very successful without those "flagship" appearances. Trust us! Plus, did you know that a lot of the books purchased in bookstores end up getting returned? And did we mention that Borders went out of business?

Yeah, we're not nuts about the traditional publishing/PR model. Also, if you're self-published or are with a more "indie" type press, Big Bookstores and the media are even LESS likely to give you a second look (until you sell 100,000 copies of your book with no help from them—THEN you're a news story!). The truth is, these "old school" type PR methods are not that effective at selling books, which is why we've saved them for the end.

THE PRESS RELEASE

Many writers want to know if they should do a press release. The answer is: Do NOT do a press release if all you have to say is: "I wrote a book." Your friends, family, and followers already know that, and the public at large frankly doesn't care.

Wow, that was harsh! Sorry—we are all about telling it like it is.

Now, if you can make your expertise (or "angle") newsworthy, you should do a press release. Media outlets want news; they need it to feed the masses yearning for information. But you may have noticed by now that the masses are typically hungry for blood, not books. So, while we don't recommend you go out and commit a crime, there are ways you can make what you have done interesting enough that you at least stand a chance of getting picked up by the news media.

Some ideas:
- Does your book tie in to a holiday, anniversary, or an upcoming event?
- Are you an expert in something that could be related to a news story?
- Does your book feature a controversial topic?
- In writing the book, did you do something unusual or noteworthy?

Here are a few actual examples of news headlines based on books (that probably started as press releases):

Taboo Topic Addressed: Historical Novel About Passing
> The idea of passing as white was never more dangerous than immediately following the Civil War.

Recession Can't Keep Seattle Author Down
> During today's era of uncertain financial times, would you quit your job to follow a dream?

Social Media for Writers: Get in There and Prove Them Wrong!

Notice that none of these say "I wrote a book!" Rather, they are newsworthy on their own, or comment on culturally relevant events. Bottom line—if you're going to write a press release in order to get a reporter to write a news story about you and your book, make sure it's newsworthy. Remember, reporters are writers too—do something to interest them, already!

If you wrote a great press release but want to pay someone to get it out there, you have a few choices: some that cost money, and some that don't. In general, when people talk about "putting something on the wire" it involves a fee. If you used a press agency to write your press release, they will probably offer you their "wire service" and probably their "clipping service" for an additional fee. Some of them are worth it, and some are not. Unless what you have written is REALLY newsworthy, the answer is most likely not worth it. (A wire service distributes the release, while a clipping service tells you who picked it up and where it has been distributed.)

So, what are your best options if you want to put it out there and don't want to pay to do it?

- Pitchengine (www.pitchengine.com) is a free site (one live release per month for 30 days). This site is really geared for social media sharing so it gives you all kinds of cool features like a dedicated URL, a shortened URL, a tweet that is pre-generated, etc. You can upload your release, multiple pictures, and just about anything else you could want someone to have about you in order to publish a really great article, which all makes it super-easy for the press to pick you up. If you decide you want the release out there longer, or plan to publish many of them, their paid service is very reasonable.

- PRLog (www.prlog.org) is a press release distribution service that offers free and paid distribution. They also have some good articles on writing press releases. If you want to get a basic release out, this is a good service. Write the release (or pay them to write it for you), pick the level of coverage you want, and voila! Distribution!

Traditional PR

Traditional PR agencies can cost big money, and it's often been our experience that they don't yield great results, especially for first-time (or fiction) authors. That said, you are perfectly within your rights if you would like to hire one, and here is a whole directory of them:
http://www.odwyerpr.com/pr_firms_database/
We also have used this "pay for performance" agency with success:
http://www.emsincorporated.com.

Before you hire anyone, make sure you do your research!
- Get references, and actually contact them.
- Be sure they have worked with authors before.
- Be clear on your agreement: What will happen if they don't get you on TV or radio as promised?
- Ask for a firm timeframe.
- Ask that they give you details about who they will approach on your behalf.
- Lastly, not all TV and radio is created equal. Be sure you are targeting the right audience.

Radio: A "Do It Yourself" Option

If you're a "do it yourself" type and want to start pitching yourself for radio shows/podcasts and you have a newsworthy story, make sure your website is in order (no, we're never going to stop saying that), get an inexpensive media directory (like http://idealady.com/article/mlist/), and start emailing or calling producers. You can do it! After all, you wrote a book! You are persistent, at the very least. Here are some other resources where you can find shows to pitch yourself:

http://radio-locator.com/
http://dir.yahoo.com/news_and_media/radio/programs/
http://www.podcastalley.com/
http://podfeed.com

As with the press release scenario, there are some things to think about before going this route.

- Do you have a story beyond "I wrote a book"? Figure that out before you reach out to producers.
- Are you an expert in something?
- Are you well suited to being on the radio or television? Being a media personality or expert is very different from being a writer!
- Does your book tie in directly to some sort of community effort or geographic region?

Radio is actually a great option for writers, especially with the increasing popularity of the e-book, where a good interview can lead thousands of people to your website, where they will instantly find your book, buy it, and start reading! If you're interested in going more in-depth with pitching yourself for these types of shows, we recommend Alex Carroll's "Radio Publicity" course. Check it out at:
http://bookpromotion.com/radio.

The "Bookstore" Book Tour

The traditional book tour (like the traditional book store) is rapidly becoming a thing of the past (with the exception of celebrity appearances). The fact is, book tours have never been responsible for selling large numbers of books. But if it's always been your dream to do a book tour (or even a reading), definitely put the feelers out to make that happen! We want you to have every author experience that you want.

Here's how to do it. If your book has been released through a traditional publisher, there is a chance the publicist there will work with you to put together a small book tour by reaching out to the bookstores on your behalf (they will probably also ask you to do some of this legwork on your own, like reaching out to stores in your local area or in cities where you might have a connection). It is unlikely that your publisher will be willing to pay for a book tour, so be sure to organize tour stops around places you might already be going or that are driving distance from your home.

If you are self-published or your book is out through a smaller press, you will need to take the reins yourself and start arranging bookstore appearances if you want this to happen. Do not be discouraged if bookstore people won't talk to you—just smile and move on. Don't let their attitudes get you down! Remember, Borders and booktour.com both went out of business in 2011. Reach out to independent bookstores, let them know about your book, and be sure to emphasize that you can bring in a large crowd of people. Do this first for all the bookstores in your local area, then start branching out to cities where you know a lot of people. Repeat until you book tour dates, and be sure to arrange to have copies of the book there for your signing, even if you have to bring them yourself.

The "Non-Bookstore" Book Tour

Depending on your topic and level of resourcefulness, you can put together a fun series of events where you can socialize, sign, and sell books. Who needs a bookstore for that?

To help you get your head around a non-traditional book tour, here are a few tour stops /speaking engagements we've helped authors with recently:
-   Book fair at a local school.
-   Author appears as kick-off speaker at a local resort's summer speaker series.
-   Reading at a local café that supports artists (this was an away trip, but was drivable).
-   Book signing at author's hometown restaurant—one she worked in through high school (another drivable distance). Also, we scheduled this during the weekend of her high school reunion, so there was good traffic that actually cared whether she succeeded!
-   Book fair sponsored by the bookstore in her hometown (same location as above). A table was very cheap and they agreed to keep some of her books afterwards on consignment in the bookstore.
-   Book party at a local wine bar.

Other authors have been quite successful as guest speakers at various events relating to the topic of their book. As part of their deal with the program host, they get their books into the gift shop or sales table for the event.

If you want to do appearances, now is the time to get creative! Start brainstorming—where are you going in the next few months that you can schedule an event? Do you have the ability to be a speaker? Are you going to any school or group events where you can request a table? If you schedule one event that is not in your immediate area, try to find a few more you can do while in that locale.

Here's an example: You wrote a guide/cookbook for people who are learning to be gluten-free. Instead of calling up all the Barnes & Noble stores where they actually have "official channels" for book signings, why not start with local vitamin stores/health food stores, libraries, or doctor's offices who might actually know of people or groups who WANT that information, and do your reading/book signing there? Your book signings and appearances will go much better (and you will sell many more books) if you take your information to the people who actually want it, rather than making them come to the bookstore.

Bottom line: Don't set yourself up for frustration by assuming you have to do a book tour the way they've always been done. Think outside that box! Everything in the publishing industry is changing, so you can think of yourself as a pioneer.

Go on a Blog Tour

Blog tours have in many ways replaced the traditional book tour altogether. A blog tour is a set of stops where you set up "appearances" to publicize your book. Most often they are on book blogs, but really they could be anywhere. The reason this is potentially more interesting than simply doing an individual guest post is that the blog "stops" on your tour typically will post the schedule on all the participating blogs. This serves to advertise your presence to each blog's unique followers, hopefully garnering you and their blog additional attention.

Also, the goal should be to do a wide variety of posts, so that people will be encouraged to stop by the "next stop." You might have a book review on one, a topic-specific guest post on another, a book excerpt on a third, a book giveaway at the fourth, and so on. Many blog tours require commenting or linking on one or more posts to earn extra entries, and/or qualify for a giveaway prize, which can be a way for all concerned to build up new followers.

So how do you set up a "Blog Tour," you ask? You have two choices: Do it yourself, or hire someone to do it.

If you do it yourself, the process is simple, albeit a little labor intensive. Using your notes from Chapter 3, as well as bloggers you've been in regular contact with through your networking efforts, you email blogs that you think are a good fit and ask if they will review or feature you and your book in some way. Keep in mind, people are going to be more inclined to visit multiple "stops" if you vary the feature type and don't just do 10 reviews in a row! When they agree to your request, ask them what fits into their schedule, and add it to your list. Once you have a list that is a respectable length (at least 10 stops) over a reasonable number of dates, you have—TA-DAA!—a Blog Tour! Simply post it to your own blog and begin publicizing it to your social media network. Most of the bloggers will also mention that they are part of a blog tour if you ask them to, which then helps to publicize their blog more widely while helping your overall participation as well.

If you decide to hire this out, there are many services online that will assist you with this for a fee. You are paying for help with setup as well as access to their network of bloggers, but you will still have to do the actual writing yourself (of course!). Because the popular blogs receive so many requests to be featured, it can be challenging to get yourself scheduled, so start early, and make sure you let the company know if you have specific requests. Identify your target blogs, and then do some research over and above the list that they come up with. The tour organizer will usually have their own website where you will find information on being included, fees, etc.

Here are some services that we know have gotten good results for authors:
- Pump Up Your Book
  http://pumpupyourbook.com
- Chick Lit Plus Blog Tours—again, the specialty is obvious here.
  http://chicklitplus.com/services/blog-tours/

Happy touring!

Book Bloggers

There are thousands of book bloggers online today. You can find book bloggers fairly easily by looking in the many online book communities, such as Goodreads and Amazon. Most book bloggers include their name (or the name of their site) and a link to their website or blog in their signature. They are also readily found on Twitter, searching on the hashtag #bookbloggers or #bookblogs.

http://bookbloggerdirectory.wordpress.com/
http://bookblogs.ning.com/

Wow—who knew, right?

Now that you have found some, what do you do with them? Most book bloggers focus on a genre, so the first thing you want to decide is whether this particular blogger is a good fit for your book. Your goal is to get good reviews and notices, so finding someone who is likely to enjoy your book is the name of the game. Read their other reviews for hints to their particular interests. Here is what you do next:

- Be sure this blog is a good use of your resources. Check their Alexa rank, follower count, activity, and frequency of posting on Twitter. Most will want a free copy of the book if they do agree to review it, so you want to be sure it is worth it before you contact them.
- Read the review policy on their website. Be sure you fit within their criteria before you contact them.
- Contact the blogger through their chosen medium—this will also be listed on their website. Some book bloggers get thousands of inquiries, and you'll stand a better chance of actually being reviewed if you play by their rules.
- You might also offer to let them give away a book as part of the promotion. Many bloggers who may not have time in their schedule to review your book will still be open to featuring you in this way.
- Offer them an interview, a guest post, or a book excerpt. Again, even if they do not have time to read and review your book, they may still want new content, so other offers like this are frequently appreciated.
- Follow up! Many bloggers receive a lot of requests, and it is easy for yours to fall through the cracks. Keep a list of whom you contacted and when, so you can easily follow up. This list will also come in handy for your next book so you can start with people who were responsive the first time around.

Getting Reviewed by Mainstream Media

Chances are you've gotten some reviews on Amazon and Goodreads by now, and if you're with a traditional publisher, they've probably sent ARCs (Advanced Review Copies) to their media contacts. If your book is reviewed by the larger media outlets (like Publisher's Weekly or BookList), your publisher will let you know, or you'll start seeing the reviews appear in your Amazon listing (under Editorial Reviews). This is more of a legacy way to promote a book, so we recommend that you not spend too much time worrying if you can't get BookList to review your book.

Note: You will probably not be able to get to them yourself if you're not with a big publisher, so if this is something that's important to you, we recommend you hire one of the publicists/PR firms in the Television, Radio, and Publicists/PR Firms section and have them approach these outlets on your behalf.

If you are trying to get more local media to review your book, we recommend looking in media directories like the ones below for book reviewers, starting with media outlets (such as newspapers and magazines) in your own town. Look for the name of the book reviewer, and make sure that reviewer is still listed on the website—remember, the newspaper industry is also in trouble! Reach out to the reviewer via email prior to sending out a review copy. Useful sites:

http://www.mondotimes.com/
http://writersmarket.com

You'll need to become a paid member in order to see their extensive database of publication, but it's well worth it for the wealth of information and updates they've collected. Look up "Newspapers," then find the book reviewer and reach out to them.

Media Bistro has a wealth of good information, including several exhaustive lists of reviewers, publishers, and agencies:

http://www.mediabistro.com/galleycat/best-book-reviewers-on-twitter_b11136

Book Clubs

Book clubs are usually comprised of readers who choose a book to read as a group, and then meet to discuss it. In the past these were affiliated with bookstores and libraries, but in recent times there has been a lot of expansion to more of a community and interest group approach (such as a particular genre). You may be surprised to find how many of your friends and family members are part of a book club, so don't forget to ask!

Note: If you are working with a book club that is an extension of a bookstore or library organization, one of the key criteria will be that your book be available via that organization, so make sure to check availability and arrange as needed!

Things you might want to do with book clubs once you find them:
- Send an email asking if they would like to read your book.
- Offer them an in-person Q&A session if you are local, or a Skype session if you are not. Skype or other online mediums allow authors

to communicate with the book club in a live format from a remote location.
- Offer special content like a short story or article that pertains to the writing of the book or the topic itself. Book clubs love exclusive info!
- Offer to send them autographed books, book plates (stickers that go in the front of the book), or bookmarks.

Asking your personal network is a good place to begin, but here are some additional online resources.

Readers Circle

This is a non-profit group that facilitates book clubs and reader circles (a reading group where everyone reads different books, but while hanging out together). They have a listings database, most of which provide contact information. You will need to email each independently.

http://www.readerscircle.org/index.html

Goodreads

Many book clubs establish a corresponding group on Goodreads. Since you are now a Goodreads member (right?), you will be able to find them there. Many of the groups are easily found by searching on genre, or geographic location—and in fact, Goodreads will even suggest book groups for you to join based on your bookshelf (another reason to get on Goodreads!).

www.goodreads.com/group

Here are some other directories where you can look for book clubs:

www.bookclub.meetup.com

www.readinggroupguides.com

www.litlovers.com

http://dir.yahoo.com/arts/humanities/literature/organizations/reading_groups/

www.loft.org (This site is hyper-local for Minnesota, but claims book clubs with several hundred participants. It's also a good example of what you can find if you do a local search—a lot of libraries nationwide are maintaining lists of their local book clubs.)

Paid Book Club Services

As a last note on this topic, there are a few websites out there that are positioned as resources for book clubs to use in order to select books. They usually offer author interviews and other things that book clubs may wish to avail themselves of, and some do giveaways. Almost all of these make their money by charging authors a fee to be listed and/or represented in their newsletters and on their websites. Some of them have better distribution than others, of course. We have tried a few of these and have seen no measurable result, so we can't recommend this method.

Every success story involving a book club that we have heard of starts with someone referring someone else. Build that network so YOU can get that referral!

Old-Fashioned E-mailing

Maybe you met a blogger or reporter at a party, and you need to follow up. Maybe you're going to pitch yourself to a magazine (and if so, good for you!). Whatever the case, you will need to make sure that any and all emails about yourself and your book are concise, informative, and attention-grabbing, so that they stand the best chance of being read.

We know, you're a writer, you love to write, and we love that about you, but let's be honest—in order to get the most bang for your emailing buck, you're going to need to get right to the point when you email someone, especially if that person is a reviewer or someone you just met.

Here are some little **dos and don'ts** for you, so you can craft an email that compels people to stop what they're doing and open it.

When sending email to people about your book, DO:
-   Indicate why you are sending the email. This not only encourages people to open your email and read it, but it also makes it easier for them to find it later in their inbox.
    Example: Book Review Request—YOUR BOOK TITLE
-   Grab their interest. Why should they keep reading? How is your email different than the other 100 emails they got today?
    Example: "My book uncovers the truth about coffee—everyone should have this information!"
-   Tell them why you are emailing them, and how it relates to you or your book. This lets them know you are not just spamming a list they are on, and creates a sense of connection.
    Example: "I chose your blog because I saw you have reviewed the book 'Morning Coffee' by Cuppa Joe, which I found inspirational when I was writing my own novel." Or "I follow you on Twitter, and see that you regularly mention coffee, as

well as books, so I thought my book might be of interest to you."

- Link to websites that contain further information, but tell them what the link directs to.

    Example: "Here is a link to a recent blog post I did on the value of coffee with breakfast," or "Here is a link to a fantastic review I received on Goodreads."

- Be concise. Delete every word that is not absolutely essential. Emails that are too long are hard to process and are much more likely to get moved to a different section of the inbox—the "When I Have More Time" section. This section is also sometimes known by its other name—the trash.

- Use bullet points or numbering. It is easy for lists to get lost and look overwhelming. Overwhelming is never good!

When sending email to people about your book, DON'T:

- Use crazy fonts, colors, or formatting. You never know how they will be reading your email (i.e. webmail, Outlook or smart phone) so it may not read the way you intend it to. Similarly, watch how often you use bold or italics.

- Use "academic"-sounding words or lingo. You don't need to prove your intelligence, and the last thing you want to do is alienate the potential reviewer by making them have to Google something you said. Yikes!

E-book Newsletters

E-book Newsletters help promote the available titles on the various eReaders with a particular emphasis on bargains and what they consider to be hot titles. Sponsoring an e-book newsletter is a great way to get exposure to a captive and avid audience of readers.

Just so you know, these newsletters don't fall within the "book blogger" or "reviewer" sections because they are pay-for-inclusion, so they technically qualify as advertising. While they can't guarantee you'll be on the New York Times Bestseller List tomorrow, e-book newsletters are an excellent way to get exposure to the right audience. And with the right mix of other promotional tools used, this can be a great boost for sales.

Newsletters have been around in various forms since the beginning of time, so what makes these newsletters so different?

Short answer: These particular newsletters are actually emails, and these emails are dedicated to specific e-book formats like Kindle and Nook. These e-book formats have very devoted subscribers, and these subscribers are especially interested in inexpensive or free content. This can be an excellent way to get yourself seen by thousands (or tens of thousands, or hundreds of thousands) of new readers, some of whom will become your loyal fans for life.

Two examples of this newsletter phenomenon are Pixel of Ink and Kindle Daily Nation. Both have large/broad reaches, and they have similar pricing structures. Depending on your budget (of course), a sponsorship with one or both of these is definitely worth a shot.

Here is a little overview of each service, just in case you're curious. Be sure to check out the websites and sign up for the newsletters (they're free), just so you know what your sponsorship would look like.

Pixel of Ink (pixelofink.com)

Pixel of Ink features daily publishing of Free and Bargain Kindle Books including Limited Time Offers, Popular Classics, and Bargain Kindle books—those that are highly rated (4-stars and up) but sold for the bargain price of under $5.

According to their website, Pixel of Ink receives over hundreds of thousands of visitors per month. They have over 335,000 Facebook Fans, plus thousands of email subscribers. Many books that have been featured have seen immediate success in both number of sales and increased sales ranking on Amazon.

There are a few requirements that must be met if you would like to reach the powerful audience Pixel of Ink has to offer, and not all books will be accepted for sponsorship. The site also clearly notes that sponsoring a post on Pixel of Ink does not guarantee sales or success of your book, so it's important to keep in mind that the benefits of the other promotional tools still apply, even if your book is featured in the newsletter.

Kindle Nation (kindlenationdaily.com)

If you have a book that is available on Kindle, a Kindle Nation sponsorship can be a good way to bring that book to the attention of their readers. As with Pixel of Ink, sponsorship isn't promised to "pay for itself," but they do guarantee a great deal of exposure, which can give a good book a chance to connect with readers.

Editorial decisions are also made based on the editors' sense of the interest among readers, but if for any reason your book isn't chosen for sponsorship, Kindle Nation's website says they will refund your payment in full. The only rigid requirement of sponsorship on Kindle Nation is that your Kindle edition must be priced at $9.99 or below, since the Free Book Alerts are all about helping readers find great reads that are also great bargains.

The website urges authors to remember that the combination of a $2.99 price and a well-targeted marketing campaign (as well as a 70% royalty) may help to turn your book into the kind of easy impulse buy that can help it to climb the bestseller list in its category. Kindle Nation reminds authors that the sponsorship will have the best impact if the book has received some reviews before the sponsorship occurs.

There are nine sponsorship options, ranging from a free book alert sponsorship to the "eBook of the Day," and you can get information and pricing for all of them here: http://kindlenationdaily.com/authors-and-publishers-how-to-sponsor-kindle-nation-daily-2/

You can also schedule a sponsorship in advance to help you reserve a date and plan a campaign for a book that is yet to be released.

The most important thing to remember on these sites is that people are making a purchase decision immediately, without doing much thinking, so you need to make it very easy for them to click that buy button! Here are a few tips to make sure you maximize your investment:

- When advertising in any sort of newsletter or online promo, have a catchy first sentence that indicates the type of book you are promoting. If you do not specify this, most publications will pull it from the back cover copy of your book. But beware, they have the right to make changes and editorial decisions, so be sure you know what your promo text will look like or at least specify how you would prefer it!

- Be sure you have at least 10 reviews on your e-book site of choice before going live. People trust other readers over you and feel comfortable knowing other people have shelled out money for your words before they did.

- Consider pricing carefully. Just from experience, we've concluded that there is a mental ceiling to impulse buys. In e-books, it appears as if that level is around $2.99. People are willing to "take a risk" for less than $3. Above that, you will need to really have a compelling number of reviews, a stellar recommendation from a well-known person, or some other factor working for you. For traditionally published authors, pricing is probably going to be beyond your control, but it's worth a conversation with your publisher if you think they're open to the discussion.

That's it! The end of the book on marketing a book! Not so complicated, right? Write a book, set up a website and some social media, then blog, post, tweet, repeat. Do this every day, add in a side of book club appearances, book bloggers, Goodreads activities, and one or more of the hundred other opportunities we've covered here, and you'll end up not only selling books, but forming a habit of marketing that will serve you through the launch of this book—and on through the rest of your career.

Good luck, and congratulations, again! Writing a book is a huge deal. We are proud of you, and hope that you're proud of yourself.

Now, go out and tell the world!

Bonus Material

More than you ever needed to know about many, MANY forms of feed management and social media!

Now that you've got your website and main social media set up, you've probably found a comfortable working structure that allows you to get yourself out there with your expertise, and building your following in a natural way that allows people to organically find your website (and buy your book). But, in case you are curious about the many, MANY more types of social media sites out there and what they do, here is a more comprehensive list.   This is the kind of thing we talk about all the time over on http://bookpromotion.com , so come on by and check it out!

Syndication

You'll want to make sure each blog post you write goes out to the most platforms possible. But how do you wire it all together? If you didn't like HootSuite (the first thing we recommended in the website/blog section), here are a few other options:

If This Then That (IFTTT.com)

If This Then That (IFTTT) is an online service that allows users to connect various platforms and channels to streamline life online. When you're managing a bevy of social networks, blogs, a Dropbox, Evernote, and checking the weather online it can be downright exhausting, if not a full-time job in and of itself. So IFTTT was created to help ease that process. Basically you tell IFTTT what to do and it does it via what's known in the service as "recipes." And all of it is based on phrase, "if this, then that" – "this" being a trigger, "that" being an action. So you can set it up that "if" you are tagged in Facebook "then" you will get a text message notifying you. While Facebook can be configured to give similar results on your smartphone, the benefit of IFTTT is that you can manage ALL these type of things in one place. And you can make more elaborate recipes that will allow cross-platform posts and tags to take place automatically without you lifting nary a finger to your computer. When combined with information sources that you check regularly it can be quite powerful. The bottom line for authors, especially authors who have built up massive social networks and online interactions, is that IFTTT can make life a little easier and save you some time so you can spend your time promoting your book and getting your next best seller ready in the wings.

TwitterFeed (twitterfeed.com)

Twitter Feed is a free service that will automatically take any post you publish on your blog and tweet it for you. It is basically a way to promote your blog without requiring any additional work on your part.

Twitter Feed can be used to post to more than one Twitter account and you can assign one Twitter Feed account to more than one blog. Users can choose the frequency rate, set up how the posts are displayed on Twitter (with or without a snippet of the blog post), and can also include a prefix to the blog posting. This tool is an easy way for authors to keep their Twitter account current. And because tweets are easily shared and spread online with the click of a button, you can garner a larger readership of your blog, and ultimately, your book.

Dlvr.it (dlvr.it)

Dlvr.it provides a way to instantly syndicate content and expand your reach on the social web and into new channels. Their tools enable you to manage and measure the flow of your content wherever your audience is at.

Dlvr.it publishes your media, your blogs, and all of your content to your social channels so that your audience can see it instantly. You can automatically or selectively update your various social networks (including Twitter, Facebook, and LinkedIn), get statistics on where your content is getting the most attention, and distribute an unlimited number of RSS/Atom feeds to your social networks.

Item updates are checked every 15 minutes or you can post on your own schedule by entering the days and times you want new items to be checked on for delivery. Dlvr.it also does a lot of work for you beyond just distributing your feed, which allows writers the opportunity to deliver consistent brand messaging for book promotion. Their service can find and replace/remove text to fine-tune the wording of your posts, automatically add hashtags to every tweet, route your content to particular social networks, and customize your short links with your own branded domain.

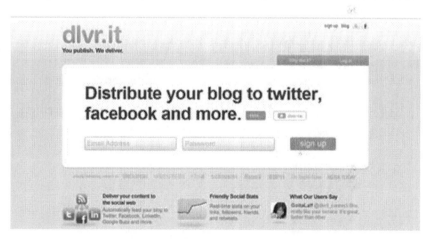

SOCIAL BOOKMARKING

Social Bookmarking helps internet users find and keep track of articles, blogs, and websites that interest them by providing a way to organize, store, manage, and search for bookmarks online from any computer.

For authors, social bookmarking can help make web content (blogs, articles, web pages) more visible and provide an additional internet community to interact in and build a following—especially useful when the time comes to share reviews and articles about a new book release.

Features such as rating systems, comment areas, the ability to import and export bookmarks from browsers, emailing of bookmarks, web annotation, and groups or other social network features are available on several sites.

Many social bookmarking services also provide web feeds for their lists of bookmarks organized by either most recent, trending topics, or subject categories.

One of the best benefits of social bookmarking services for authors on a mission to get their book out there is that they level the playing field for promotion. A site that's obscure but interests many people can be spread quickly and rise to the top of the heap.

Digg (digg.com)

Digg is a social news site that gets its "news" from lists of popular stories being shared across the web. Users submit news articles, videos, and stories, and then vote on or "digg" their favorite ones.

Digg buttons are available on articles and websites all over the web, and writers can easily add these buttons to their own online content. By clicking on these buttons, users share the content with their friends and others. Those clicks are tracked, and the number of people from the Digg community that have "dugg" that story is displayed on each article with a Digg button.

The number of diggs a story collects over time can affect how that story spreads. The most popular stories of the moment are promoted to the Top News section of the web site. Items can be sorted by most recent or what's trending right now.

Personal news feeds can also be created, corralling stories chosen specifically for the user based on the people they follow, the stories they read, and the stories that are trending across the entire Digg community.

Digg is also integrated with Facebook, so users of both can connect their accounts, allowing Digg articles to be shared on the user's Facebook page.

Delicious (delicious.com)

A social bookmarking service, Delicious lets users save all their bookmarks online, share them with other people, and see what other people are bookmarking. The most popular bookmarks being saved are then categorized into areas of interest, and on the Delicious home page you can see the most popular bookmarks in real time.

Delicious keeps all your bookmarks in one place, stored online so they can be accessed from any computer. Search and tagging tools help users keep track of their entire bookmark collection as well as help find new bookmarks.

The service also includes various tools for social bookmarking, such as browser buttons for saving bookmarks for any browser, the ability to add your bookmarks and tags to your website or blog, and badges that encourage people to bookmark your website or blog.

Additional tools include a "tagometer badge" that shows the tags and number of bookmarks for your pages, and a playtagger for MP3s which allow audio files to be bookmarked. You can share bookmarks with your friends on Delicious, Twitter, or email.

StumbleUpon (stumbleupon.com)

StumbleUpon acts as a filter to direct users to websites which are relevant to their personal interests. So rather than searching for quality websites through the vast amount of information available on the internet, StumbleUpon members are taken directly to websites matching their personal interests and preferences among the nearly 500 topics featured on the site.

The participation of community members helps maintain a database of the most current and best quality sites. Old or low-quality sites are actually removed from StumbleUpon if their ratings become too low.

The StumbleUpon Toolbar is integrated with your browser to allow for one-click access to quality websites. A simple two-level rating system (thumbs up/thumbs down) gives users the opportunity to pass on or give their opinion on any webpage with a single click, and these ratings connect people sharing unique combinations of interests.

The site rating system not only helps recommend the site to others, but fine-tunes your experience with StumbleUpon as well. Increasingly relevant content is delivered to the user through a toolbar which tracks what the user has liked in the past.

SOCIAL MONITORING

As your presence in the social networks grows, the work involved in keeping those networks maintained increases. Your presence online won't mean much unless it drives people to action with a reply, a retweet, a comment, or a click. And people won't do that unless you're interacting with them.

Social monitoring services help do some of the work of social networking for you by tracking the conversations and interactions that are happening on the web which somehow involve—it could be somebody deciding to follow you on Twitter or sending you a message in Facebook.

So to make sure you can spend your time writing more best-sellers, these monitoring services take on part of the job of interacting on the social networks and, by doing so, help you maintain a good reputation online.

Overall, using a social monitoring service is a great customer service touch for your fans and an automated way to manage your network of followers.

Social Oomph (socialoomph.com)

SocialOomph is a service that provides free and paid productivity enhancement services for social media users. Base features include the ability to schedule tweets, track keywords, promote yourself with extended Twitter profiles, save and reuse drafts, and maintain a personal status feed. And you can mute annoying tweeters, forward direct messages, and hide tweets you've already read on Twitter. The service also helps you comb through your @replies (which ideally will increase with people tweeting about how much they love your book) with a Replies Daily Digest.

An additional fee applies for features like auto-follow and auto-direct message (which allows you to follow and respond to those who are reaching out to you automatically). There's also an automated unfollow feature so you can stop following those people who have decided to stop following you.

Additional fee-based features available in the professional version include tools for freeing up time and increasing productivity, such as scheduled status updates, wall updates, and various secured features.

Klout (klout.com)

The Klout Score is the measurement of your overall online influence. Klout uses over 35 variables on Facebook and Twitter to measure True Reach, Amplification Probability, and Network Score to create scores ranging from 1 to 100. Higher scores represent a wider and stronger sphere of influence.

The scores aren't just important to understand for your own knowledge of how successful your online promotion of your book and yourself as an author is, but also for others to realize the same. People tend to pay attention to those with clout—or "klout." So get familiar with the three measures of online networking success as defined by Klout: True Reach, Amplification Score, and Network Score.

True Reach is the size of your engaged audience and is based on those of your followers and friends who actively listen and react to your messages. Tracking the results can help you create interesting and informative output to build an audience.

The Amplification Score measures the likelihood that your messages will generate actions (retweets, @messages, likes and comments). By understanding if your tweets are sparking conversation, you will have the ability to create content that compels others to respond and spreads into networks beyond your own.

Network score indicates how influential your engaged audience is based on actions such as retweets, @messages, follows, lists, comments, and likes with the belief that every time a person performs one of these actions it is a testament to the authority and the quality of your content. The final Klout Score is a representation of how successful a person is at engaging their audience and how big of an impact their messages have on people—which, at its core, is the goal of everyone who picks up a pen or hacks away at their laptop at all hours of the night to write a book.

Twitter Counter (twittercounter.com)

Twitter Counter bills itself as the top site for Twitter statistics. The site provides statistics of Twitter usage and displays them in powerful and easy to understand graphics. Spots are also sold on the website for people who want to gain more followers—which for some authors might be the way to go to either begin or increase their following.

Twitter Counter also offers a variety of widgets and buttons that people can add to their blogs, websites, or social network profiles to show recent Twitter visitors and number of followers.

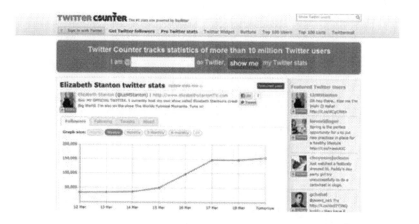

The Twitter Widget shows you which Twitter users visit your site or blog. The code can be copied and pasted from the Twitter Counter site to be displayed on your own website.

TWITTER CLIENTS

Though the less technically inclined among us might believe that Twitter Clients are people that Twitter invites to meetings to help woo their business, it's basically just a fancy way of saying "app" or application. And when it comes to Twitter, there's definitely "an app for that" all over the web. Sorting through them can be a little tough—it's a fresh field for developers, and some of the apps are Twitter-approved while others are unofficial. But it's worth it to find a few that work for you in order to make your tweeting life easier.

TweetDeck (tweetdeck.com)

TweetDeck is a personal browser that allows you to connect with your contacts across Twitter, Facebook, MySpace, LinkedIn, and more. Available on your computer desktop or mobile phone, TweetDeck allows you to customize your Twitter experience with columns, groups, saved searches, and automatic updates.

The idea with this, as with most applications related to social media, is to help you stay updated with the people and topics you care about in the easiest way possible. In the midst of book promotion, the more you can simplify other tasks, the better. TweetDeck allows you to see what people are saying about you and join the conversation by tweeting, sharing photos, videos, or links directly from TweetDeck.

You can also connect with your Facebook and MySpace friends directly from TweetDeck by updating your status, posting photos or videos, commenting, and liking. TweetDeck groups your friends to make it easier to follow only those whose activity you really want to see by creating columns for each of your groups of friends.

TWITTER FOLLOWER MANAGEMENT

Now that you've accrued a decent-sized following on Twitter, how are you going to manage your followers to get more when you need them and kick the inactive ones to the curb? Management software, of course!

Twitter Follower Management sites and services track your users for you, tell you who's doing (or not doing) what, and also help you accrue more followers if that's your goal.

Though getting rid of followers may seem counterintuitive, it's actually a good idea to keep spammers out of your social networking crew and maintain a group of active, engaged followers. Those are the people who will actually help spread your message, and their actions help keep your online influence up to snuff.

UnTweeps (untweeps.com)

As a writer, or anyone who takes their social networking seriously for promotion, the number of tweeps you follow is a valuable commodity to your Twitter presence, so the idea is not to waste that resource on people who aren't engaging with you. UnTweeps uses the Twitter API to unfollow selected people you are following. UnTweeps uses Twitter's login system which then allows UnTweeps to work on your behalf.

After logging in, you can enter the number of days in the past you want to check. If you enter 30, then anyone who hasn't updated their Twitter status (tweeted) in the past 30 days will be shown on a list. Then, with just a simple click, you can unfollow those who have been inactive.

If you are following people who don't tweet very often, but you still want to follow them, Untweeps gives you the option of adding them to the whitelist—this prevents them from showing up every time you do a search to see who hasn't been tweeting lately.

Pro features are available for those who want to use UnTweeps more than three times per month. The subscription cost is $5 per month. The paid subscription also lets you use UnTweeps Pro on unlimited accounts.

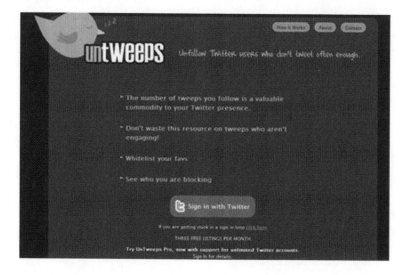

ACKNOWLEDGMENTS

LORI

Special thanks to Stephan Cox, Ken Culwell, Jim & Jan, Andrea, Katherine, Heather, Lana, Dave, and my community of friends on Facebook and Twitter as well as those who keep reading my blog and laughing.

KATHERINE

First and foremost - Lori, you rock! Second, I couldn't do what I do, without the Booktrope crew - Ken, Heather and Andy. Special thanks to Tess Thompson, Jesse James and Terry Persun. And really, to all the authors who work with me, thank you - without the books, the rest doesn't mean much. Last but never least - to the Fye and Sears clans, who knew books would be important someday, so listened patiently to my blathering all along.

Made in the USA
Charleston, SC
15 May 2013